The

MAGAZINE WRITER'S
Handbook

Writers' Bookshop

This ninth edition published in Great Britain, in 2002, by
Writers' Bookshop, an imprint of Forward Press Ltd
Remus House, Coltsfoot Drive, Woodston,
Peterborough PE2 9JX.

First published by Allison & Busby Ltd 1985
Reprinted 1986
Second edition published 1987
Third edition published 1990
Fourth edition published 1992
Fifth edition published 1994
Sixth edition published 1997
Seventh edition published 1999

Eighth edition published 2001 by Writers' Bookshop

ISBN 1-902713-15-X

Edited by: Ann Johnson-Allen
Cover Design by: Mark Rainey
Page Layout by: Mark Rainey

CHRISS McCALLUM & GORDON WELLS

The
MAGAZINE
WRITER'S
Handbook

Writers' Bookshop

9th Edition
2002/3

Other relevant books by Chriss McCallum:

Writing for Publication (How To Books)
Getting Published (How To Books)

Other relevant books by Gordon Wells ...

from Writers' Bookshop:

How to Write Non-Fiction Books
Writing is ... Fun! (for children)

from Allison & Busby:

The Craft of Writing Articles
Be A Successful Writer: 99 Surefire Checklists

CONTENTS

INTRODUCTION

To be successful in the highly competitive business of writing for magazines, you need to know what to write, how to write it, and who to write it for. In other words, you need:

- for fiction writing, a powerful imagination

- for non-fiction writing, knowledge of a particular subject (or knowledge of where to find out about it)

- the ability to communicate your thoughts clearly, in language your readers will understand

- knowledge of where and how to sell what you write.

In this handbook we focus on that vital last point – we aim to help you find the right markets for your work.

Of course, no handbook can replace the need to study the market for yourself. Any reference work like this is likely to be out of date in some details even before its publication date. In such a volatile business as magazine publishing, change is inevitable. This is particularly true these days. As the recent closure of well-established titles like *Woman's Journal* and *Woman's Realm* has shown us, longevity is no guarantee of survival.

Use this handbook as a 'first sift' of the market-place, a foundation on which to build your own market research. Study the reports and look at our method of analysing each magazine; see how we draw up as complete a picture as possible of its content, its target readership *(see below)*, its editorial requirements, and its potential as a market. These reports provide a model to enable you to move on and study other magazines when you venture beyond the necessarily limited choice we show here.

Thorough study of the magazines you want to target will greatly increase your chances of success. Writing for magazines is a highly competitive business. It has always been, as it is now, a buyers' market. There are far more writers trying to get published than there are openings for their work.

This handbook will show you how to get to know the market and the people you want to write for. Study it well – it will give you a priceless edge over the countless numbers of writers who pepper the market with random submissions instead of taking aim with a carefully targeted piece of work.

The Choice

There are several hundred magazines and newspapers published regularly in Great Britain and many of these accept material submitted by freelance writers. This handbook looks at a selection of magazines likely to be the most interesting to the freelance writer. The choice of publications in the main part of this handbook has been based on the following considerations:

- the publication's willingness to consider freelance submissions
- no need for specialised knowledge or qualifications
- no need for localised knowledge
- payment for publication.

These considerations have led to the exclusion of specialist trade, profession or hobby publications. Who but a pharmacist could write for *The Pharmaceutical Journal* or an aeromodeller for the *Aeromodeller* magazine? And there are many such publications. Of course, this is not to suggest that a freelance writer should not try writing for such publications as *The Pharmaceutical Journal* if he or she is a pharmacist by profession. Far from it. You should always 'work to your expertise' – there's less competition there. But a pharmacist will probably know the journal well and will not need the 'first sift' market study that this handbook offers.

Similarly, any freelance writer based in Cheshire will know *Cheshire Life* county magazine and be more able to contribute to it than someone living in Cornwall or the Scottish Borders. Any freelance writer who particularly wishes to contribute to a remote county magazine should buy a copy anyway: no handbook will do away with that need.

In further justification of the carefully limited scope of this handbook, we remind the reader of the wisdom of Samuel Johnson, who pointed out that 'no man but a blockhead' would write without prospect of payment. There is little point in studying a market that does not offer an opportunity to recoup the cost of that study.

The choice of magazines for inclusion in this handbook was based on the considerations listed above. The resultant list can be classified under three headings:

1. Women's magazines: overall these are the biggest magazine market, particularly for short stories, but also very much for non-fiction work. (There is a growing tendency though for the women's magazines to prefer commissioning non-fiction themselves – often from ideas generated in-house – rather than choosing from piles of unsolicited submissions. And many magazines now require prior consultation in the form of a query and/or synopsis before any submission, even of fiction.)

2. General interest magazines: these are becoming something of an endangered species these days. The tendency in the magazine world for some time has been towards specialisation – seeking to appeal to a niche readership. Many of those that remain tend to be the 'countryside' glossies, or those of that ilk. These are not always the best of payers. Within this category though, there are some of the more widely read women's magazines too, such as *The Lady*.

3. Leisure interest magazines: although specialist magazines have largely been excluded, we assume that many writers know at least something about doing things in the house and garden, about cars and trains and holiday travel – and a bit about writing. We have widened the scope a little to include a few such magazines. (And, because many non-fiction writers also illustrate their work, the biggest weekly photographic magazine has been included.)

Some of the publications investigated in detail in this handbook accept no fiction; others accept no non-fiction. All of those examined are prepared to consider 'writer-initiated' fiction or non-fiction ideas from freelance writers without editorial 'pull' or the benefit of a famous name – ordinary writers like us. The reports included in the handbook are all based on personal study of the magazines; they are not just editors' blurbs.

For this new edition, the study reports have been thoroughly revised on the basis of fresh sample copies of the magazines; many have been completely rewritten. Some of the less relevant magazines have been dropped to make room for new and/or better freelance markets. Generally, though, we don't include new magazines until they are reasonably established and look likely to survive. (A writer cannot extract payment from a magazine that has ceased publication.) Each of the reports has been checked with the appropriate editor and then *factually* corrected where necessary.

Payment

One of the most important things for a freelance writer to know about a magazine is how much the editor will pay for a writer's work. It is not enough merely to know that the editor *pays*; is the payment *enough*? Does the hire fit the labour? Freelancers must decide for themselves whether they are prepared to invest the work needed to research, write, and perhaps also illustrate a feature article for a mere £50, or for a more generous £150, per thousand words. Yet far too many editors still prefer not to disclose this vital and basic information to writers in advance. (Obtaining advance information about payment is one advantage of the preliminary outline approach so often now required.)

However, rates of payment are a variable feast: editors will give more for one piece of work than for another, and pay a better rate to established contributors than to new ones. Basic rates tend to increase over the years. Accordingly, all payment rates are quoted only by broad groups. Payment rates have been assessed or determined from a number of sources: personal experience, published figures, or a general 'feel'. In all cases, editors have been shown the draft reports, including the assessment of payment rates, and have had the opportunity to amend or correct them.

Payment rate groups are listed on page 16.

Readership

To sell freelance material to magazines you need to give the editor what she/he wants. You can only do this with any confidence if you have a clear idea of the magazine's readership. If a magazine is directed at teenage girls, it is pointless to try to sell the editor a short story about a grandmother's problems with her two-year-old granddaughter. Even if the story were brilliant, the editor would not be interested because the magazine's readers would not *identify* with the characters.

The easiest way for a freelance writer to build a picture of the typical reader of any magazine is from the advertisements. Advertising agencies know the media well; they do not advertise their products in a magazine whose readership will not be interested in them.

For that reason, the magazine studies in this handbook include an appraisal of the advertisements as well as of the editorial pages. This appraisal is not in terms of A/B/C1/C2/D type readership – which means much to an advertising man, but little to the average writer – but is in more emotive, meaningful terms. 'Up-market' is not a precise term, nor is 'mail-order shopper', but you can readily picture a readership from such descriptions. The readers' average age, too, is often less than precise: advertisers need this precision, but writers do not.

Some magazines produce media packs that indicate their typical/target readership. It's worth contacting the publicity department of a magazine you would like to write for, to ask if such a pack is available. You could also look at the magazine's website – and most magazines have one nowadays – where a good deal of this kind of information is given.

(Many magazines also produce an editorial calendar, detailing their planned schedule of contents over the coming months. This calendar is intended to interest advertisers, but they might be willing to send you one if you ask politely.)

Most of the market-study reports include brief details of a few recent feature articles that the magazine has carried. These are useful in two ways:

- they indicate the range, or type, of feature that the editor is (or has been) interested in using, and in that sense serve as a model for future submissions

- they also provide the freelance writer with ideas for articles on similar subjects that might be offered to other magazines. You don't need to worry about plagiarism in 'lifting' such article ideas; the end result will inevitably be very different from the original – and there is no copyright in ideas, only in the way they are written up.

The market study reports also include details of the regular columns carried by the magazine. These are important to the freelance writer for the simple reason that the editor is most unlikely to accept a feature article on a subject usually reserved for the columnist, who is probably paid a regular retainer.

Changes in this Ninth Edition

Since the publication of the previous, eighth, edition, the magazine market has continued in its now customary state of flux. New magazines are launched, some survive, some die young; older ones cease publication. Editors move around, titles are bought and sold ... Each new edition of this handbook reflects those changes.

The following magazines, which were included in the 'Market Studies' section of the eighth edition, have been dropped. They have either ceased publication (or been merged into other titles), are no longer prepared to consider unsolicited material from freelance writers, or are now, in our view, an insufficient market for 'ordinary' writers.

Bunty *(now monthly and using only archive material)*
Country
Home & Family
The Illustrated London News
London Magazine
TV Quick
Wild About Animals
Woman's Journal
Woman's Realm
World Wide Writers (incorporated into Writers' Forum)

(It is most regrettable to have to record, above, the 'departure' of one of the few publications dedicated to publishing short stories.)

The following magazines, either new or newly 'discovered' (or 'rediscovered') by the authors, have been added to the 'Market Studies' section:

Autocar
Country Walking
Essentially America
Eve
Focus
Girl Talk
Ireland's Own
Junior
Making Money
Prospect
The Railway Magazine
Wanderlust

And, of course, all of the magazine 'reports' have been carefully reviewed, updated and rewritten. (They are all based on an assessment of the opportunities for writer-initiated material – i.e., a freelance writer has offered the editor an idea and got a go-ahead, even if only tentative.)

In this edition, I have incorporated in the body of the reports the coded and abbreviated information previously contained in a box at the top of each report page. Only two pieces of information are now still in coded form: the circulation figures and the payment rates, the former because of ever-changing numbers, and the latter because editors are reluctant to commit themselves to specific payments but happy to endorse a (fairly wide) band of figures.

Previously noted changes in the overall magazine 'scene' have continued, including, particularly, the growing popularity of the 'short-short', or 'coffee-break' story and the enormous increase in the use of readers' 'real-life' stories. (And these personal experiences really are true stories; several magazines insist on names and addresses and permission to take photographs before accepting any story. This is very different from the 'Confession' stories of some years ago – which were merely 'true-to-life - sin, suffer and repent' first person fiction.)

It is noticeable, too, that still more magazines are specifying 'no unsolicited submissions' in their mastheads – usually in extremely small print. The work of sifting out a few acceptable articles and short stories from much that is unpublishable is becoming increasingly uneconomic.

The only way for the freelance writer to get around this is to submit advance queries, mentioning or showing copies of your published work, and either follow up with a quick phone call or ... accept that you will often not get a reply. Luckily, there are still some publications – often the lower-paying ones – that will consider the work of beginners; and there are always the local, specialist and hobby-based publications for the beginner to sharpen his or her teeth on.

The 'literary' and 'small press' magazines are combined in the chapter entitled 'Alternative/Independent magazines'. For easy reference, a common format has been adopted for all these entries. The list is far from complete – the world of small magazines changes even more rapidly than that of 'mainstream' publications – but it is a useful introduction to an interesting world.

Further Benefits in this Edition

Thanks to the technology now available, we are able to offer, for the first time, an e-mail update service, free to readers of this edition. See Chapter 12 for details.

Finally, elsewhere in this handbook are several short sections on a variety of subjects of interest to the magazine writer. These include advice on how and where to get in touch with fellow writers with similar interests; an extended reminder of how to submit work to editors (which should be common knowledge, but is the sort of thing that editors repeatedly feel the need to advise writers about); and some elementary advice on writing picture stories. There is also a chapter – expanded from the previous edition – on the delights of the Internet, suggesting websites likely to be of particular use to writers, and listing a few websites to introduce you to writing for electronic magazines (e-zines).

The Future

Readers – writers and editors alike – are invited to write to the authors, c/o Writers' Bookshop, with any information that will help with the e-mail update service and with future updates of the market study reports (and any other items) in this handbook, so that we can make future editions even more helpful. The authors would also like to take this opportunity to thank those who commented on earlier editions, or sent information on these and other publications. (If you write to the authors by post, and would like a reply, please enclose a stamped addressed envelope.)

Finally, our thanks are due to all the editors of all the magazines who responded so quickly and encouragingly, and who commented so helpfully on the draft market study reports. The accuracy of the reports owes much to the editors; responsibility for any residual faults rests at the authors' doors.

1

THE MARKET STUDIES

The next seventy-odd pages, in this chapter, contain the real meat of this handbook: the detailed market study reports of those magazines we consider to be the best, most likely outlets for ordinary freelance writers. As already explained, the studies do not include specialist trade or hobby magazines or county magazines.

The magazine reports are in alphabetical order, and the pages are set out to a common format. At the top of each page, the magazine's title with, below it, any message included in their masthead or on the magazine spine. Below this comes the name of the editor and, where useful/available, the names of the features and fiction editors. The next line gives the group by which the magazine is published, followed by the editorial address, phone and fax numbers, e-mail address and website details where applicable.

Next comes a paragraph showing the magazine's frequency and price, its circulation band, the year it was founded, the kind of material it wants (and doesn't want), whether a query is required prior to submitting material, and the likely level of pay it offers.

The text of each report also follows a broadly standard sequence of information: target readership, make-up of the magazine (advertising and editorial content), regular sections/columns, typical potentially freelance-contributed features and stories, editorial requirements/specifications, and opportunities for fillers etc.

The tables below show the circulation per issue and the pay rates likely to be offered to freelances:

Circulation per issue:

a	=	up to 50,000
b	=	50,001 to 100,000
c	=	100,001 to 300,000
d	=	300,001 to 800,000
e	=	800,001 and above

Lowest pay per 1,000 words:

A	=	£1 to £40
B	=	£41 to £60
C	=	£61-£100
D	=	over £100

ACTIVE LIFE

The lively magazine for the years ahead

Editor: Helene Hodge

Lexicon Editorial Services Ltd, 1st Floor, 1-5 Clerkenwell Road, London EC1M 5PA. Tel: 020 7253 5775. E-mail: activelife@lexicon-uk.com

Website: www.activelifemag.com

Every two months, £2.50. Founded 1989. Circulation c. Publishes non-fiction and short fiction. Query advisable for features. Pay band C, at the end of the month of publication.

As its title suggests, *Active Life* is a lively publication – its target readership the 'grey panthers', young-in-heart adults of 50-plus years, and of both sexes. (The actual core readership is probably nearer their early sixties.) The Editor describes the magazine's 'house style' as 'Daily Mail-speak – short and punchy, nothing too long or boring to read.' The over-50s are a prime readership target everyone wants to reach.

A typical issue of *Active Life* has 84 colourful saddle-stitched pages of which about 40 per cent are adverts – the advertisers know how to reach their audience. The adverts are widely varied but with travel opportunities, clothes, pharmaceutical products, financial services, charities, stair lifts and recliner chairs predominating. As well as the formal advertisements, there are competitions and reader offers, and many free giveaways.

On the editorial side, much of the magazine is divided into regular sections or departments: money, law, travel, well-being (health and fitness) interests, practicals – which includes cooking and gardening – and people. Within those sections there are many actual or potential freelance-contributed features, as well as obviously staff-written pieces. Each issue has two or three such features, including travel features.

Active Life usually includes an interview with a celebrity of appropriate age. (Sir Paul McCartney and Jane Seymour were the subjects in the issues we read, and the interviews were bylined to members of staff.)

In one issue we reviewed, topics covered included, among others, keeping in touch with your grandchildren via the internet; 'Flushed with Pride', a visit to a new museum of sanitary ware; and a freelance written (I recognised the writer's name) travel piece on dream destinations for a special anniversary. Another issue we read had two travel features, one on New Zealand, where *The Lord of the Rings* was filmed, the other on Malaysia; in the same issue there was an article about a couple with a flourishing new career running a village post office. There was also an article about milestones. All these features included informative sidebars.

The Editor particularly looks for a strong 'hook' to start each piece. It's wise to check interest in a feature before submitting it – query first with a brief outline. Good photographs will undoubtedly increase your chances.

There is a short story in each issue of *Active Life*. This should be around 1,200 words 'on a theme relevant to the readership'. One of the stories in the issues we read was humorous, the other slightly 'spooky'.

There's a lively Letters page using 5 or 6 letters per issue, the best (only) getting a prize.

Tip: Contributors' notes are available – send an s.a.e.

AMATEUR GARDENING

Simple advice for superb results

Editor: Tim Rumball

Editor's PA: Janet Salisbury

IPC Country & Leisure Media, Westover House, West Quay Road, Poole, Dorset BH15 1JG.

Tel: 01202 440840. Fax: 01202 440860.

E-mail: amateur_gardening@ipcmedia.com

Website: www.ipcmedia.com

Weekly, £1.30. Founded 1884. Circulation b. Non-fiction only – *don't send fiction or poetry*. Pay band D, at the end of the month of publication.

Amateur Gardening is a lively IPC weekly targeted at keen gardeners, most of whom will have ample basic gardening knowledge but are always eager to learn new ways and means. The full-colour magazine focuses on topical gardening articles and expert advice, much of which comes from well-known gardening personalities like Charlie Dimmock, Bob Flowerdew, Pippa Greenwood and Monty Don, among others.

A typical issue of *Amateur Gardening* will have about 52 saddle-stitched A4 pages of which 7 or 8 will be advertisements, mainly for plants, seeds, garden equipment, gardening books and the like. There are regular pages devoted to news, advice on problems, reader offers and competitions, and a gardener's crossword with a £15 cash prize. There's also a 'Swap Shop' where readers can advertise (free) their plants, seeds and surplus tools for sale or exchange.

Within the magazine's regular departments/sections there are many freelance contributions – but mostly from a 'stable' of tried and trusted experts (many, as mentioned above, well-known TV and radio 'names'). There is, though, no reason why an experienced journalist should not contribute successfully. If you have a *relevant* topical and practical idea, write to the Editor with details. There's a 'Reader's Garden' feature, which could be an interview. (In the issue we reviewed, this feature was supported by eight images.)

Features are strong on facts and supported by sidebars listing contacts, addresses etc. and/or step-by-step instructions. Required length for features is up to 1,000 words.

Every feature article in the magazine is profusely illustrated, always in high-quality colour. All images must be pin-sharp, preferably using Fujichrome Velvia transparency film.

'Newsdesk' is a six-page feature welcoming news items. Call Mark Rosenberg on 01202 440848, fax: 01202 440860 or e-mail: marc_rosenberg@ipcmedia.com

The 'Postbag' uses more than a dozen letters (some back-issue-related) and gardening tips per week (50 to 150 words); published letters earn a £5 garden gift token (£10 with a photo), the Star letter wins £20 and Tip of the Week wins £10.

Tip: If you have ambitions to contribute features to *Amateur Gardening*, the letters/hints page would be a good place to prove that you know your stuff. Get your name known.

AMATEUR PHOTOGRAPHER

Editor: Garry Coward-Williams

Editor's PA: Christine Lay

IPC Country & Leisure Media Ltd, King's Reach Tower, Stamford Street, London SE1 9LS.

Tel: 020 7261 5100. E-mail: amateurphotographer@ipcmedia.com

Website: www.amateurphotographer.com

Weekly, £1.95. Founded 1884. Circulation a. Non-fiction only. *No fiction or poetry.* Pay band C, at the end of the month of publication.

Amateur Photographer covers every aspect of photography for a readership of keen photographers of all ages, from beginners to professionals.

A typical issue has 100 highly illustrated saddle-stitched pages of which about half are adverts. A vast amount of the ads will be for photographic dealers, listing cameras etc., plus several display ads for new cameras, digital photo scanners (complete with associated computer software), new lenses and the latest colour film; and pages of classifieds offering second-hand cameras and other equipment.

Editorially, every issue has many pages of news, views, equipment tests and summarised specifications, and several advice columns. Virtually all the magazine's regular pages are staff-written, but there are opportunities for photographers expert in any field to provide one-off technique articles on all types of photography. Of course, you must know your stuff. Approach the Editor with an outline of your proposed feature – don't send a complete ms till you get the go-ahead.

Aim for a finished length of 1,000-1,500 words. Picture captions should be supplied on a separate sheet.

There's also an opinion column, 'Back Chat', inviting 'Your thoughts or views on photography' (about 600 words).

Readers' letters: There are about half a dozen sometimes back-issue-related letters each week, the 'Letter of the Week' winning £110-worth of Kodak film, all others printed receiving a free roll of Kodak film.

Photographs: Readers are welcome to submit photos for 'Portfolio', which shows the work (from 2 to 5 photos each) of four photographers in each issue. Captions must be supplied giving the location and details of camera, lens and film used for each photograph.

Tip: The Editor advises that there is no scope for words without pictures.

ANTIQUES & COLLECTABLES

Editor: Diana Cambridge.

Merricks Media Ltd, Charlotte House, 12 Charlotte Street, Bath BA1 2NE.

Tel: 01225 786800. Fax: 01225 786801.

E-mail: edit@antiques-collectables.co.uk

Website: www.antiques-collectables.co.uk

Monthly, £2.60. Founded 1998. Circulation b. Non-fiction only. *Don't send fiction or poetry.* Pay band C, at the end of the month of publication.

Antiques & Collectables is a beautifully produced glossy magazine with 100 colourful, profusely illustrated perfect-bound pages of which 30 or so will be adverts – mainly for antiques shops/centres and art galleries. Its target readership embraces collectors of all ages with interests in every field of antiques and collectables.

Editorially, there are several regular sections: art and antiques news; a diary of upcoming auctions and fairs; internet news; collectors' clubs addresses; a price guide section giving estimated and achieved prices at auction; 3 pages of 'private sales' adverts; a prize crossword.

The Readers' Letters page offers a bouquet from Bed of Roses for the Star letter.

The Editor will consider ideas for photo-features on any specific area or subject of antiques and collectables, whether dealing or collecting, length 1,000 to 1,500 words. Photographs must be top quality, preferably transparencies but really pin-sharp prints can be used.

Here are a few examples of the subjects *Antiques & Collectables* has covered, to give you an idea of the magazine's enormous scope of interest: 'Living with Arts & Crafts', 'Dream Beds', 'All About Susie Cooper', 'Spaceabilia' – collectables inspired by the moon landings, 'Collecting Cross Stitch', decorative tiles, Moorcroft, 'Modern Studio Pottery', 'Bristol Blue Glass', telephone boxes, jukeboxes, Wade pottery, Wedgwood china, sofas and settees, pressed glass, washstands, umbrellas and walking sticks, classic cars, football programmes ...

All features must include informative sidebars detailing: points to watch, care and repair, further information, further reading, relevant websites, price guide, collections to visit and so on. There is nothing vague about any feature in *Antiques & Collectables*. You really need to know your subject.

Book reviews: *Antiques & Collectables* will carry an occasional book review from a reader. If you would be interested in reviewing, e-mail your details *briefly* to diana.cambridge@merricksmedia.co.uk

Comprehensive guidelines are available – the Editor asks that you send for these (s.a.e., please) and study them carefully before you submit your ideas. Don't send complete features, as the magazine might well have covered the subject too recently for your piece to be considered, or might have something similar already in the pipeline.

Tip: It would be advisable to study several issues before sending a query or outline – you can order recent back issues through the magazine.

AUTOCAR

Editor: Rob Aherne

60 Waldegrave Road, Teddington, Middlesex TW11 8LG.

Editorial tel: 020 8267 5630.

E-mail: autocar@haynet.com

Weekly, £2.10. Founded 1895. Circulation b. Non-fiction only. Query (with synopsis) essential. Pay band C, mid-month following publication.

Autocar is a general interest motoring weekly offering high quality content to its knowledgeable car-enthusiast readership. *Autocar* publishes features on all aspects of cars, motoring, and the motor industry. Coverage includes road tests, motor shows, motor sport – national and international – and descriptions of new cars.

A typical issue of *Autocar* will have about 130 profusely illustrated perfect-bound pages of which about one-third will be advertisements. The ads, as you would expect, are for cars and motoring accessories, insurance services and the like. The display ads are mainly for new products from major car companies, and there's a 'Classified' section with ads for every car-related product and service you could possibly need, plus 'For Sale' and 'Wanted' ads. There are also pages of new car prices and a motoring website directory.

On the editorial side, every issue of *Autocar* has four or five main features, half a dozen news reports, and three or four detailed reports on new cars, including fact files and performance analyses. There's a lively Letters section using 10 or 11 letters and awarding a prize for the best each week, a motoring 'agony uncle', prize competitions and a Trackday Diary.

Most of the features in *Autocar* are written in-house or by regular specialist contributors. However, the Editor will consider *relevant* ideas from knowledgeable freelances. If you can offer a better-than-competent illustrated feature, especially if it focuses on an unusual but clearly car-related subject, you could have a good chance of success.

One of the issues we reviewed had a feature on stunt driving, 'School of hard knocks', about the Los Angeles stunt academy that teaches you to drive like Mel Gibson. Another issue profiled 'The man who can': 'gamekeeper turned poacher' Nick Freeman, a former prosecutor for Greater Manchester Police who is now famed for getting people like David Beckham and Sir Alex Ferguson acquitted on speeding charges.

Features are usually 1,000 to 2,000 words, but don't send complete mss – approach in writing with ideas/synopses only. Photographs should be high-quality colour, and *Autocar* accepts digital media.

Autocar is also interested in news items and tip-offs, and exclusive motor industry photos, especially of pre-production models under test.

Tip: Get to know the magazine well before you offer anything – the Editor receives too much unsuitable material.

BELLA

Editor-in-Chief: Jo Sollis

Features Editor: Sue Ricketts

Fiction Editor: Linda O'Byrne

H. Bauer Publishing, Academic House, 24-28 Oval Road, London NW1 7DT.

Tel: 020 7241 8000.

Weekly, 66p. Founded 1987. Circulation d. Publishes non-fiction (Real Life stories only) and short fiction. Pay band D, at the end of the month of publication.

Bella is a bright, breezy, much illustrated and very colourful weekly magazine for women of all ages – but particularly those in their late twenties and early thirties. A typical issue of *Bella* has about 60 saddle-stitched pages of which 9 or 10 will be advertisements – mainly for food and pharmaceutical products.

On the editorial side, each issue of *Bella* includes a number of regular sections, covering fashion, beauty-care, cookery, home-making, and bringing up children. There are pages on legal matters, financial concerns, readers' rights, health and fitness … and news of soap personalities and other 'celebs'. There are also astronomy and 'agony' columns.

There are several Real Life stories in each issue. In common with other similar magazines, the Real Life stories in *Bella* are well paid, and completely factual, although names are occasionally changed. Some of these stories, however, are written 'as told to …' with a writer's name in the byline, so if you hear of a good local story, you might be able to interest the Features Editor. The people involved must be willing to have their photographs appear in *Bella*.

Bella prints two short stories in every issue. One is a 2,000-word two-pager, often a romance but always told with plenty of warmth, conflict and strong emotional depth – with a 'nice-feeling' ending. The other fiction spot is a one-page short-short story, 1,000 to 1,200 words long. *Bella* also welcomes submissions of short fiction for their seasonal 'Specials'.

Detailed study of several copies of the magazine is recommended. Contributors' guidelines are available for fiction (send an s.a.e.). Address stories to Fiction Editor Linda O'Byrne – and don't expect decisions in less than about six weeks.

The magazine welcomes letters, tips etc. Include your name and telephone number in case they need to get back to you. Write to the above address or e-mail bella.letters@bauer.co.uk

- 'We've got mail' – 5 or 6 letters each week, £50 for the Star letter, £25 for the others.
- 'Blush with *Bella*' – embarrassing moments, 60 words, £50.
- 'Rat of the Week' – about 150 (true) words plus photo - £150.

BEST

Editor: Louise Court

Fiction Editor: Pat Richardson

National Magazine Company, 197 Marsh Wall, London E14 9SG.

Tel: 020 7519 5500. Fax: 020 7519 5516. E-mail: best@natmags.co.uk

Weekly, 66p. Founded 1987. Circulation d. Publishes non-fiction (True Life stories) and short fiction. Pay band D, at the end of the month of publication.

A bright and colourful weekly launched in 1987 by leading German publisher Gruner + Jahr and bought in 2000 by the National Magazine Company, *best* is now well established on the British scene. A typical issue will have 60 much-illustrated saddle-stitched pages of which about a dozen are advertisements, for food (for people and pets), holidays, pharmaceutical products, special offers etc. The magazine is intended to interest women of all ages, but its core readership is likely to be women in their late twenties and early thirties, probably with jobs outside the home.

On the editorial side, *best* is, inevitably, in a somewhat similar mould to its competitors – True Life stories and plenty of reader participation. Regular sections/pages include fashion, beauty-care, health, fitness, and home-making. There are 'soap' updates, travel, several pages of recipes, consumer news, a horoscope column, and an 'agony' column. There's a page about 'this week's people', with 'the gossip, the glamour, the soaps, the scandals'. Two or three crossword variant competitions, with good prizes, feature in every issue. Most issues also contain some sort of feature (profile or interview) about a current celebrity, and one or two spectacular news stories.

There is little scope for the 'ordinary' freelance non-fiction writer – unless you either have (and are willing to reveal) an unusually interesting life, or can find an intriguing local real life story which might suit being written up as a 'As told to ...' feature. True Life stories pay £250 each – but they really are true stories, not made-up ones.

For short-story writers, though, *best* is a good market: each issue has a one-page 900-1,000-word short-short story. These don't have to be romances or 'twisters' – just good, well written, 'not instantly transparent' stories. The Fiction Editor likes stories that are fresh and lively, with a young outlook – no OAPs or middle-aged housewives – sexy but not explicitly so, and set in modern situations. Stories can include romance, revenge, mystery, comedy, the supernatural, unexplained or paranormal – but absolutely *no* animal narrators, murdering spouses, lottery stories, or 'twin characters' mix-ups.

Comprehensive guidelines for short story submissions are available; send an s.a.e. – you could increase your chances by reading these carefully, along with a thorough study of several issues of the magazine.

Letter- and tip-writers too can do well with *best*. Regular slots are:

- Letters: 'You tell us': 8 or 9 per issue, up to 150 words each, £50 for the best, £25 for the rest. Address to Eithne Heveran, Letters Editor.
- '10 new tips to make your life easier': 10 per issue, each 15-30 words long, £15 each (photographs not asked for). Address to 'Tips'.
- 'Star Pic': one snapshot each week, £30.

BEST OF BRITISH

Past & Present

Publisher & Editor-in-Chief: Ian Beacham

Bank Chambers, 27a Market Place, Market Deeping, Lincs PE6 8EA.

Editorial Tel/Fax: 01778 342814. E-mail: mail@british.fsbusiness.co.uk

Website: www.bestofbritishmag.co.uk

Monthly, £2.75. Founded 1994. Circulation a. Non-fiction only. *Don't send short stories*. Pay band A, at the end of the month of publication.

Best of British is, as its title implies, a celebration of all that's best in Britain ... including a high proportion of nostalgia. Its readership tends to be mainly mature/elderly men and women.

A typical issue of *Best of British* has about 70 much-illustrated and colourful saddle-stitched pages. Of these, about half-a-dozen will be advertisements, mainly for books, CDs, videos, walk-in baths and 'back-care' chairs, plus several reader offers. An interesting 'Helping Hands' regular feature carries queries, requests, announcements etc., free of charge; you can search for a long-lost pal or find a pen-friend here. There's also a list of events taking place in the current month.

Best of British invites readers' memories for a regular section, 'Yesterday Remembered'. Contributions of up to 1,000 words are welcomed (with relevant pictures, which are returned). Those published earn £20. The issue we saw had seven of these memories, including 'Tasting the NAAFI', camping with the Boy Scouts in 1947, and an appreciation of the MG Magnette.

There are eight pages of readers' letters – no payment or prize offered. There are also a few pages of news items, headed 'Britain now ...'.

Most interesting to the freelance writer, though, are the one-off illustrated articles on British heritage past and present, with a strong focus on people and nostalgia. Many *Best of British* features are staff-written, but the Editor is 'happy to consider for publication articles of up to 1,200 words provided as manuscripts or on disk (in Microsoft Word RTF format). Submissions have a far better chance of being used if accompanied by relevant black and white pictures or colour transparencies.'

Guidelines are given in the masthead.

Publication cannot be guaranteed, and material may be held for up to six months. You can send the complete feature, but it might be better to submit an idea and outline first. In either case, be sure to enclose an s.a.e.

Examples of topics covered in one issue we reviewed are: the Cockney Pearly Kings and Queens; 'Big Game fishing ... off Scarborough!'; penny arcade machines on Brighton Pier; the sinking of HMS Hood; ghostly goings on in a signal-box in Hampshire half-a-century ago. There's also a regular feature titled 'My First Job' – the one we saw was about 'a life on the railways'.

Tip: The Editor prefers illustrated articles taking a positive view of particular aspects of Britain and our heritage, British people's passions, humorous pieces on relevant topics, and (especially) interviews with celebrities talking about what they love about Britain.

BROWNIE

Editor: Marion Thompson

The Guide Association, 17-19 Buckingham Palace Road, London SW1W 0PT.

Tel: 020 7834 6242.

E-mail: MarionT@guides.org.uk Website: www.guides.org.uk

Monthly, £1.40. Founded 1962. Circulation a. Publishes non-fiction and short stories. Pay band B, at the end of the month of publication.

Brownie is a bright and breezy monthly magazine for Brownie Guides – that is, girls aged 7 to 10. It has been going for more than 40 years and has certainly kept up with the times.

A typical issue of *Brownie* will have 32 saddle-stitched pages. Only one or two pages will be advertisements, for charities and for fun days out. The whole magazine is produced with colourful zest - there's barely a hint of white paper throughout.

Brownie is full of profusely illustrated double-page spreads, including a centrefold with an animal poster and a pop poster on facing pages. Other spreads can be step-by-step words-and-pictures instruction (250 words, in 'steps') for fairly simple but carefully thought-out things to make with inexpensive materials.

There are short (300-400 words) factual articles written in illustrated 'info-bite' or 'snippet' form, a short story (500-800 words) about a Brownie-related activity, or a picture-story (about Super Brownie, scripted by the Editor). There are pages of picture-puzzles and giveaways, a crowded pen-pal page, quizzes, and a couple of pages of readers' letters, poems, drawings or photographs – from Brownies only. The best letter, poem etc. wins a prize. There are also occasional 'Question and Answer' interviews with teenage pop stars, with appropriate photographs.

The editor of *Brownie* particularly welcomes craft articles and sport and hobby information.

Craft articles in the two issues we reviewed included instructions on how to make decorative cushions for World Thinking Day, a heart-shaped silver-foil-covered photo frame, an Easter bunny filled with chocolate eggs, and a colourful Mother's Day vase. Each activity entailed about 6 or 7 steps, each described in about 20-50 words plus illustrative photographs and/or sketches. If you can't provide an appropriate illustration, a rough sketch will suffice.

One hobby piece demonstrated how to play badminton, and had a 'more info' sidebar.

Each issue of *Brownie* has a double-page spread consisting of up to ten 50-word illustrated snippets focused on the animal kingdom. One we saw was all about rabbits, in the wild and as pets, another showed the varied wildlife to be found in Australia.

Tip: Editorial guidelines warn against involving Brownies – in stories or how-to articles – in doing anything unsafe or dangerous, either by day or by night. They also point out the need for an up-to-date view of family life: today's Brownie could well help her dad with the washing-up and her mum in the garden.

And a brief reminder: not all Brownies are Christians; they can adhere to other religions and faiths.

CANDIS

For you and your family

Editor: Jenny Campbell

Newhall Publications Ltd, Newhall Lane, Hoylake, Wirral CH47 4BQ.

Tel: 0151 632 7642. E-mail: jennyc@candis.co.uk

Website: www.candis.co.uk

Candis, founded almost 40 years ago, is the magazine of the Candis Club. The Club exists to promote social activities and provide benefits for its members, and to bring together people who are interested in supporting medical charities for which the Club raises more than £1million a year through sales of *Candis*. (*Candis* is only available to new members on postal subscription. For a *free* copy and subscription details, e-mail postal@candis.co.uk or call 0870 745 5656 and then press 3, or write to Candis Subscriptions, FREEPOST at the above address.)

Monthly, £2.50. Circulation d. Publishes non-fiction and fiction. Pay band D, made after publication, a month after your invoice.

Candis is in A5 format, typically having 138 saddle-stitched pages, of which about 16 will be advertisements – for assorted products like pharmaceuticals, decorative figurines, personal jewellery, videos and books. There are also many Candis Club offers of holidays, luggage, plants, insurance and the like. There is a slight emphasis throughout on health-related features and sections – understandably so, bearing in mind the Club's charity donations.

Editorially, *Candis* has many regular sections including Candis Club news, antiques, cooking, gardening, knitting, relationships, consumer affairs, the environment, and numerous competitions; two regular 'name' columnists (Laurie Graham, Polly Toynbee); two celebrity interviews, one 'conventional', (Cilla Black, Alan Titchmarsh, for example), one a conversation over a lunch table, 'Out to Lunch' (typical subjects Terry Waite, Jonathan Dimbleby).

'Reader to Reader' has 3 or 4 letters, each winning a £10 gift voucher.

Each issue has several one-off features on a wide variety of topics, typical subjects being: the remaking of 'The Forsyte Saga', 'Born Liars' (how human beings have evolved by deceiving each other), a (Christmas) visit to Hamley's toy shop in London, 'Make Art Not War' (a report from Mozambique), and 'Enchanted Places' (was Middle Earth based on Birmingham?).

All one-off features are commissioned from established writers; the Editor never accepts work or ideas from unpublished writers. However, if you can provide clips or photocopies of previously published work of the required standard, you're welcome to offer ideas, *not complete mss*.

Candis insists on a high standard of accuracy from its feature writers, and recommends keeping all research notes, tapes etc., and a record of sources. Most features will be pre-commissioned: if at the end of the day, through no fault of the writer, the feature can't be used, a 50% kill fee is paid.

Fiction: Every issue of *Candis* has a 1,000 word short story; these are usually by published authors, but occasionally stories are bought from unpublished writers. The stories are often 'nostalgic-romantic' in style but can be 'straight' or possibly slight 'twisters'. All suitable stories are considered.

Tip: Look out for *Candis* short story competitions.

CAT WORLD

Britain's best loved cat magazine

Editor: Jo Rothery

Ashdown.co.uk, Avalon Court, Star Road, Partridge Green, West Sussex RH13 8RY.

Tel: 01403 711511. Fax: 01403 711521. E-mail: editor@catworld.co.uk

Website: www.catworld.co.uk

Monthly, £2.75. Founded 1981. Circulation a. Non-fiction only. *Don't send short stories or poetry.* Pay band A, at the end of the month of publication.

Cat World is an attractive glossy magazine in its twenty-first year of publication. It's packed with super colour photographs of lovely cats – even a centrefold cat pin-up. It is a magazine for all cat-lovers with inevitably a slight emphasis on the interests of breeders and 'owners' of 'show cats' rather than ordinary 'moggies'. (Forestalling criticism, the quotation marks around 'owners' reflect our awareness that no one 'owns' a cat.)

A typical issue of *Cat World* will have 80-plus tastefully colourful saddle-stitched high-gloss pages of which about a third will be taken up with advertisements – a dozen or so pages of display ads and around 20 of classifieds. The display advertisements offer everything 'catty' – from cat litter and flea powders to cat insurance, food and charities. The classified ads are mainly taken up with directories of breeders and of studs, and a register of cats which have just had kittens (for sale).

Editorially, there are several regular features: a breed profile (in the issue we reviewed this focused on the Balinese cat); a feature on 'rescue' cats; case studies of feline behaviour, 'Cats on the couch'; a multi-expert problems section; a homeopathic cat-health page; several pages of cat show and other 'catty' news; a cat-book review column; and 'Cats on the net', websites featuring feline collectables. There is also a Letters page (inevitably 'Pawpost') using 5 or 6 newsy and sometimes illustrated letters per month - no mention of payment or prizes.

There is a regular reader-participation spot: 'Tail end', a one-page 600- to 750-word photo- or drawing-illustrated pet eulogy.

There are also several other 'non-expert' feature articles in each issue, with pictures. Recent pieces included 'Diary of a Reluctant Show Cat'; 'Love or Hate', how an irresistible kitten 'proved a Damascus experience' for a hitherto anti-feline husband; and 'In search of the British big cat', a close encounter with the 'Beast of Bodmin'.

The Editor will consider articles of 600-800 words, 1,000 words, and 1,500 words. Photographs accompanying articles can be colour prints or transparencies (35mm is acceptable).

Regarding payment, the magazine's masthead states that 'all material is accepted solely on the basis that the author accepts the assessment of the publisher as to its commercial value'.

While e-mail queries and submissions by e-mail and by disk (PC format) are preferred, submissions on paper will be considered but should be crisp, clean, clear and scannable.

Tip: The Editor emphasises how important it is for prospective contributors to *read the magazine*, to observe and absorb the tone, style and flavour of *Cat World* today.

CHAT

Editor: Paul Merrill

Features Editor: Anna Kingsley

IPC Connect Ltd, King's Reach Tower, Stamford Street, London SE1 9LS.

Tel: 0870 444 5000. Website: www.ipcmedia.com

Weekly, 68p. Founded 1985. Circulation d. Publishes non-fiction only - mainly True Life stories. *No fiction.* Pay band D, at the end of the month of publication.

A bright and breezy women's magazine from IPC, *Chat* is in direct competition with such German-import magazines as *Take a Break* (page 74) and *that's life!* (page 76). Like them, it is aimed at women of all ages but most particularly at 25- to 45-year-olds – probably working mums with school-age children and limited spare cash.

A typical issue of *Chat* will have 60-70 colourful saddle-stitched A4 pages full of pictures. About a dozen of the pages will be advertisements, for beauty and health products, pet food, mail order catalogues, finance, foods, CDs, DVDs and videos, and a full page of small ads (mostly for psychic readings and chat-lines).

On the editorial side there are many regular pages/sections covering fashion, soap and celebrity gossip, beauty care, health and fitness, cooking, and holidays. There are also 'agony' and astrology pages, with tarot, runes and a 'psychic health' guru, 'Ruth the Truth'. The pages are also packed with reader-participation competitions: arrow words, crosswords etc., with prizes like holidays, shopping vouchers … and cash.

Forming a major part of the editorial content of each issue of *Chat* are the dramatic True Life stories. There are usually about half a dozen two-page stories (earning up to £1,000 for the person concerned). Be warned, though, these really are true stories and feature photographs of the actual people – which means they offer virtually no scope for the ordinary freelance writer. (Unless your life is truly exciting?)

Note: *Chat* no longer publishes any fiction.

Chat is a particularly good 'market', though, for the writers of letters and tips. Opportunities include (and look out for new openings all the time):

- 'Blimey! That's Clever!' using about 20 tips per issue, about 15-30 words each, earning £15, £25 with a photo, and £35 for a star tip.
- 'Naughty jokes!': 25-85 words, earning £15 each.
- 'Chat Gazette': News items (What's been happening in your life?), varying lengths, paying up to £100.
- 'My spooky story': Encounters with spirits from the other side, about 200 words, earning £50.
- 'Just kidding': Pictures and stories about your little ones, paying £15 for each story used, £25 with a photo.

CHOICE

Get the most out of life

Editor-in-Chief: Sue Dobson

Features Editor: Carole Dawson

Kings Chambers, 39-41 Priestgate, Peterborough, Cambs PE1 1FR.

Tel: 01733 555123. Fax: 01733 427500.

E-mail: choice.bayardpresse@talk21.com

Monthly, £2.30. Founded 1974. Circulation c. Non-fiction only. *Don't send fiction or poetry*. Pay band D, at the end of the month of publication.

Choice is a lively and informative magazine for relatively affluent men and women of fifty and over, encouraging a positive attitude to life.

A typical issue will have about 140 colourfully illustrated perfect-bound pages, of which about 35% will be advertisements, mainly for financial services, 'walk-in' baths, health products, holidays and retirement property - plus special reader offers.

Editorially, *Choice* has many regular sections including health, fitness and beauty, relationships, gardening, cookery, travel, the environment, entertainment, with pages of news, reviews, forthcoming events, and a couple of problem pages. There are puzzles, including a prize crossword and a nostalgia quiz, and there's a reader-service section to help readers find those with whom they have lost touch.

A substantial section, 'Your Money and Your Rights', looks at pensions, investments, taxes etc. A regular column, 'Online' keeps readers up-to-date on computers and the world wide web, and there's a page about the latest technological innovations.

There's a forthright and spirited Letters page, 'Your views', with a dozen or so contributions. The 'Star letter' wins a valuable Waterman fountain pen, the others earn £5 each.

Each issue has several one-off features, some clearly staff-written or commissioned from experts, but there are openings for freelance contributions *relevant to the readership* and written in the right style. The issue we reviewed included, for example, 'Trace Your Family Tree' (with a comprehensive 'How to get started' sidebar); an interview with Babs and Robert Powell; 'When listening helps', a feature on The Samaritans; and 'A Passion for Jigsaws'.

Although most articles in *Choice* are commissioned, all unsolicited article submissions are carefully read. You would be much better advised, though, to submit an idea in writing first, with a brief synopsis plus one or two cuttings or photocopies of similar published work – and, of course, an s.a.e.

Study the magazine carefully, and make sure any ideas you suggest are appropriate for *Choice*'s readership: real-life stories, interesting people of 50-plus, British heritage, hobbies and activities, all presented in a positive, up-beat style.

If you can offer relevant photographs, preferably colour transparencies, your chances of success will be much greater.

CHRISTIAN HERALD

Editor: Russ Bravo

Features Editor: Jacqueline Stead

News Editor: Karen Carter

Christian Media Centre Ltd, Garcia Estate, Canterbury Road, Worthing, West Sussex BN13 1EH.

Tel: 01903 821082. Fax (Editorial): 01903 821081.

E-mail (Features): features@christianherald.org.uk

E-mail (News): news@christianherald.org.uk

Website: www.christianherald.org.uk

Weekly, 70p. Circulation a. Publishes non-fiction only. *Don't send poetry or short stories*. Pay band B, on publication.

Christian Herald is a tabloid-sized weekly newspaper available from Christian bookshops, by order from newsagents, and on subscription – details are in the paper and on the website.

Christian Herald is aimed at evangelical Christians, both sexes, all ages, but perhaps concentrating its attention most on 25- to 45-year-olds. Throughout, it is written in a lively, positive, bright and contemporary style – committed, but with a sense of humour. It says its design style is 'Daily Mail meets Daily Mirror'.

A typical issue of *Christian Herald* will consist of 20 newsprint pages of which the first half-dozen are filled with news, both national and world, about church and evangelical matters. Within the paper there are 4 or 5 pages of advertisements, 70 per cent classified, the rest display; it's particularly good for church-related job ads, for holiday accommodation ads, and there are always display ads for charities etc.

After the news pages come plenty of pages of features – some staff- or regular-contributor-written, and often news-related. The issue we reviewed (a March issue which had many holiday adverts) included a freelance-written feature titled 'Christian B and B – it's heavenly', in which three hoteliers were interviewed about the challenges of providing good Christian hospitality. This feature was about 1,000 words long, including 20 'expert tips' for opening and running a Christian B and B, plus 7 photographs. Under the section heading 'Childwatch', there was a piece titled 'Seeing red', a report on the plight of families on low incomes in the UK.

There are several regular features which are particularly suitable for, and open to, the religious freelance writer. These include, for example, 'Changing Church: how churches are meeting the challenge of our rapidly changing world'; 'Growing churches: stories of growing churches making a real impact on their communities'; 'Interviews: public figures and their faith'; and 'Human interest: good stories of people putting their faith into action or overcoming difficulties in their lives.' Length should be 550-700 words for short features, 800-1,000 for longer pieces. For full contributors' guidelines, including submission requirements, send an s.a.e.

There are also short reviews – of books, films, CDs, TV programmes – several of which were credited to children.

There is a lively Letters page, 'Your Say', using 7 or 8 letters a week, some back-issue-related. No payment is offered for these.

Christian Herald uses no fiction at all nowadays, so don't waste your time or theirs sending short stories.

COLLECT IT!

How to spot bargains

Editor: Gwyn Jones

Features Editor: Brenda Greysmith

Essential Publishing Ltd, 1-4 Eaglegate, East Hill, Colchester, Essex CO1 2PR.

Tel: 01206 796911. Fax: 01206 796922.

E-mail: collectit@essentialpublishing.co.uk

Website: www.collectit.co.uk

Monthly, £2.80. Founded 1997. Circulation a. Non-fiction only. *Don't send fiction or poetry.* Pay band C, at the end of the month of publication.

Collect it! is a profusely illustrated magazine for collectors of both sexes and all ages, in all fields, focusing largely (though not exclusively) on 'affordable' artefacts not yet old enough to be classified as antiques. It deals with the kind of things people collect, from toys, old bottles and limited edition plates to sporting memorabilia and Royal Doulton china.

A typical issue of *Collect it!* will have 84 colourful A4 perfect-bound pages, of which about ten will be display advertisements, mainly for collectable items, and three or four will be classified ads. There are many regular columns, like 'Collecting on the Web', 'Collectors Club Focus', 'Distinctly Dolls', and 'Collecting for Kids', among others. There are pages of news and updates from the collecting world, a 'Bookshop', holiday offers and a prize crossword. There is also, now, a regular column on collecting in the USA.

There's a page of 'Your Letters', using three or four letters, with the 'Star Letter' winning a prize; this page includes a 'Can you help?' column, seeking information on 'collectables' subjects. The rest of the magazine – about half – is devoted to one-off features. Some of these are staff-written, and though the others are freelance-written two or three bylines appear regularly. (Interpret this as an incentive to try harder – to give the Editor just what she wants.)

One-off features are almost all either three- or four-page articles, length about 1,200 or 2,000 words, and all are heavily illustrated, always in colour. On average, there are three photographic illustrations per page. The Editor likes writer-supplied 35mm transparencies, although digital media can be used. If the subject merits it, the magazine might arrange for a staff photographer to visit.

In one issue we reviewed, the wide range of topics included 'Dog Figurines', 'Golf Collectables', 'Dolls Houses', 'Be My Valentine – cards from Victorian times', 'Timmy Woods Handbags', 'The World of Wodehouse', and 'Spitting Image Caricatures'.

Each feature article incorporates anecdotes and quotes from collectors and/or experts and dealers, and includes a 'Fact File' – contacts, websites, dealers, historical information, reference books, museum shows and so on. Study several issues of *Collect it!*, to see how thoroughly each topic is covered.

It's absolutely essential to send a query first to avoid subject overlaps. Outline your idea in detail. The Editor likes to see examples of relevant published work. Material is taken for future issues, often months away. Decisions might take a couple of months.

COUNTRY LIFE

Editor: Clive Aslet

Features Editor: Rupert Uloth

IPC Media, King's Reach Tower, Stamford Street, London SE1 9LS.

Editorial tel: 020 7261 7058. Editorial fax: 020 7261 5139.

Website: www. countrylife.co.uk

Weekly, £2.80. Founded 1897. Circulation a. Non-fiction only. *Don't send short stories or poetry.* Pay band D, within a month of publication.

Country Life is an upmarket weekly magazine with a decidedly affluent readership. The readership is both male and female, probably living in the country, but certainly not strangers to the London scene either. These are mostly stately home or large country estate dwellers – and those who aspire to the lifestyle – involved in conservation, the arts, our heritage, country sports, and general good living.

A typical issue of *Country Life* will have from about 92 to 130-plus high-gloss perfect-bound profusely illustrated pages, in a format larger than A4. About half will be advertisements – mostly confined to before and after the editorial material. Usually, about two-thirds of the advertisements are for large, expensive country houses and estates; apart from one or two smaller properties, most of the houses are now firmly in the £½m-plus price bracket. Other advertisements are for works of art, antiques, furniture, garden equipment etc., plus about a dozen pages of classified ads – for property, pets, billiard tables etc.

Editorially, there are many regular pages/columns – country news, saleroom activities, reviews (books, films, music, exhibitions etc.), gardening, motoring, fashion, bridge and sports. There are on-going series like My Week, The Wild Week, News Diary, and a 'Town & Country' collection of 100- to 200-word country-interest snippets. They might welcome *relevant* contributions – contact the Page Editor, Leslie Geddes-Brown on 020 7261 6614. There is a non-paying Letters page using around eight mostly back-issue-related, sometimes illustrated letters every week – write to Correspondence Editor Polly Chiapetta, fax: 020 7261 5139 or e-mail: polly_chiapetta@ipcmedia.com

There are usually several one-off features in each issue. Many are commissioned, a number are by regular contributors or by staff writers. But there is some scope for the experienced freelance with expertise and relevant ideas to contribute. Issues we read included features on the first national festival of ponds and lakes; 'How to find a gardener'; 'The Malahide Doll's House', and 'Houses by George Gilbert Scott'.

Length varies from about 800 to 2,000 words. Illustrations are seldom provided by the writer.

If you have a *relevant* idea for a *Country Life* article, write in – or preferably e-mail - with just a 3- or 4-line synopsis. If they express interest, then follow up with an outline, plus your credentials and photocopies of similar published work. DO NOT phone for a response: they usually respond within a week or so. (They dislike unsolicited phone calls.)

But take note – around 90% of *Country Life*'s content comes from regular contributors; little unsolicited material makes the grade.

Tip: The editor looks for strong, informed material rather than amateur enthusiasm.

COUNTRY QUEST

Your Wales and Borders magazine

Editor: Beverly Davies

7 Aberystwyth Science Park, Aberystwyth, Ceredigion SY23 3AH

Tel: 01970 615000.

Monthly, £2.00. Circulation a. Publishes non-fiction and poetry. *No fiction.* Pay band A, at the end of the month of publication.

Country Quest is much like a big English county magazine but is aimed at readers throughout the whole of Wales and the border counties. (It is this broad regional interest that justifies its inclusion. Ordinary county magazines are outside our self-imposed terms of reference – see Introduction, page 7.) The magazine's readership is clear: people of all ages and both sexes, but predominantly of mature years, living in or having a particular personal association with the area.

A typical issue of *Country Quest* will have 52 perfect-bound pages, profusely illustrated in both colour and black-and-white, of which about a fifth will be advertisements. The adverts are for a wide variety of products – reflecting the readership and the firms operating within the area.

Editorially, there are regular columns and one-off articles. Regulars include local-interest book reviews, an antiques section, a feature on 'interesting' cars, a series of 'Country Curios' (a photo of a building or place of interest accompanied by an informative caption). All these are by established contributors. There's also a Letters page, four or five longish letters each month, mostly back-issue-related – no pay.

There is also a poetry page titled 'Poetry Corner' publishing three or four poems each month, invariably 'traditional/conventional' in style.

But it is for its one-off features that *Country Quest* is of most interest to the freelance writer. There are up to a dozen or so such features per issue, and almost certainly all initially unsolicited. These are all about people, places, customs, traditions and events associated with the readership area – Wales and the Borders.

Articles in the issues we reviewed included: 'The man who was always painting – Barmouth's forgotten artist' (Alfred Keeley Brazier, founder of the Merioneth Artists Society); The Duke's confession – a terrible crime from the past'; 'Welsh lovespoons – A loving tradition'; 'A genuine Welsh pirate – Sir Henry Morgan's antics on the Spanish Maine'; 'A carpenter who changed history – Nicholas Owen's priest holes'; 'Royal associations – Grosmont's links with monarchy'; and 'The Romans in Wales – Our country two thousand years ago'. As this sample selection shows, *Country Quest* uses an admirably well-balanced mix of topics.

The Editor advises that one-page feature articles should be around 700 words, two-pagers should be 1,400 words. *Country Quest* uses no fiction.

Original illustrations are welcomed: if provided, deduct 200 from the above wordages. *Country Quest* will accept black-and-white prints, or colour prints, transparencies or negatives.

Decisions come fairly quickly. Deliver/submit date-related material at least two months before issue date. All work should be sent to Erica Jones, Head of Content.

Tip: Features in *Country Quest* are concisely written and rich in facts.

COUNTRY WALKING

Editor: Nicola Dela-Croix

Bretton Court, Bretton, Peterborough PE3 8DZ.

Tel (Editor): 01733 282608. E-mail: nicola.dela-croix@emap.com

Tel (Features Editor): 01733 282611. E-mail: emma.kendell@emap.com

Monthly, £2.95. Founded 1987. Circulation b. Non-fiction only. Query essential. *No short stories or poetry.* Pay band A/B, at the end of the month of publication.

Country Walking is an attractively produced magazine targeting walkers of all ages and abilities who enjoy a great day out in the country. The emphasis is always on getting pleasure from walking and the countryside.

A typical issue of *Country Walking* will have 116 colourfully illustrated saddle-stitched pages of which about 30 will be advertisements, all related to walking: clothing, shoes, mobile phones, country parks, holidays, hotels, self-catering accommodation, mountain rescue charities ... There's a photography club, prize competitions, giveaways, reader breaks and a book shop.

On the editorial side, there are regular sections on equipment testing (fleeces, waterproof trousers, day sacks, walking poles and the like); 'Walkers' phonebook' listing useful contact numbers; 'How to ...': half a dozen or so assorted practical tips – in two issues we reviewed these included how to use binoculars properly, predict hill temperatures, draw a gradient profile, understand Scottish rights of way, avoid headaches, escape chilblains, explore wetlands, and buy the right walking pole; 'Foot notes' has news and stories from the world of walking and the countryside – in the issues we read, these included advice on avoiding crime, Britain's most impossible stile, electric fences in Lakeland, and saving the red squirrel. The 'Out and about' section picks the best walks and country events each month. There's a lively Letters page, too – no payment or prizes.

Each issue of *Country Walking* has six or seven main features. In the two issues we read these included, among others: 'Dogs on Dartmoor – four of the best hound-inspired routes on the moor'; 'Walking festivals'; 'Kick-start your spring – buy a one-way ticket on a steam train, and walk back'; 'Lake District secrets – enjoy uncrowded trails and fabulous views from the fringes'; and '10 most romantic walks – don't forget to pack the champagne!'.

Country Walking has a regular section called 'Down Your Way', a pull-out collection of 25-plus easy to follow walks 'taking you all over Britain'. These are very detailed, and include route maps and Ordnance Survey references plus a photograph (writer-supplied) relevant to the walk. Walks must be thoroughly and recently researched. E-mail the Production Editor (trevor.rickwood@emap.com) if you would like to be considered as a contributor to this section.

Very little unsolicited material is accepted, so it's best by far to offer ideas/outlines in the first instance, by letter or e-mail. Length will be discussed if your idea is taken up. An original approach to a subject will increase your chances.

Photographs should be colour transparencies or sharp colour prints. If walkers are featured they should be appropriately dressed.

Tip: We recommend a thorough study of several issues before you offer anything.

THE COUNTRYMAN

Editor: David Horan

Countryman Publishing Ltd, 23 Sheep Street, Burford, Oxfordshire OX18 4LS.

Tel: 01993 824424. Fax: 01993 822012.

E-mail: burford@countrymanmagazine.co.uk

Monthly, £1.99. Founded 1927. Circulation a. Owned by Countryman Publishing since 2000. Non-fiction only, and the occasional poem. *No short stories.* Pay band C, at the end of the month of publication.

The Countryman is aimed at country lovers, mainly middle-aged or older and fairly affluent, of both sexes, and dedicated to enjoying the countryside – although quite possibly living in the town or city. The Editor will not consider any material that expresses sentimentality about the country, is party-political, or that unquestioningly promotes field sports.

A typical issue of *The Countryman* will have about 100 much-illustrated perfect-bound A5-sized pages. There's a picture on almost every page, both colour and black-and-white photographs and the occasional pen and ink drawing. About 15 of the 100 pages will carry advertisements, including half-a-dozen pages of classified ads. The adverts, like the contents, reflect the readership: they offer country-wear, crafts, book-finding and book-publishing services, holidays and the like.

Editorially, there are several regular columns, including 'Notes from a Wildlife Garden'; 'In a Country Churchyard'; 'Curiouser & Curiouser' (a miscellany of British curiosities and personalities, with much reader input and interest); an events calendar; listings of Farmers' Markets countrywide; and a prize crossword.

There's a readers' letters section, 'Dear sir', a dozen or so contributions from readers world-wide – no payment or prizes.

Of most interest to the freelance writer are the many one-off feature articles in *The Countryman*. There are 15 or so illustrated articles in each issue. One issue we reviewed included, among others: 'The fight to save the sweet swan of Avon'; The frightening tale of Bungay's black dog'; 'A crop that has to be harvested by candlelight' (rhubarb); 'When dogs had their days in harnesses'; 'Our bloodiest battlefield' (Towton); 'Leaves and flowers mark the place' (bookmarks); and a profile of Lord De L'Isle of Penshurst Place in Kent, one of 'the businessmen of the countryside'.

If it's about the country – and well written – your article could interest the Editor, who prefers features to be around 1,000 words. Articles supplied with top-quality illustrations stand a far greater chance of being accepted. Illustrations can be colour transparencies, archive black-and-white photographs, and line drawings – and *The Countryman* can use digital media.

The Editor will consider queries/outlines, preferably by e-mail, or you can send complete features by e-mail or on disk (Macintosh, or PC ASCII or Text). Typewritten or word-processed mss will only be considered if they are crisp, clean, and sharp enough for scanning – and even then they would have to be outstandingly good to stand a chance.

Tip: If it comes down to a choice between two articles of equal interest and merit, one on disk and one not, the article on disk will be the one used.

CRIMEWAVE

Editor: Andy Cox

TTA Press, 5 Martins Lane, Witcham, Ely, Cambs CB6 2LB.

E-mail: ttapress@aolcom

Website: www.ttapress.com

Two a year, £6.00, on subscription or from bookshops. Founded 1998. Publishes short crime-related fiction only. Pay band A/B, on publication.

The UK's only magazine publishing crime short stories, *Crimewave* is a beautifully printed and illustrated 132-page perfect-bound publication in B5 format (the size of a hardback book). Every issue contains stories from top names in the crime fiction world, but editor Andy Cox finds room for quality stories from lesser known and unknown writers.

Crimewave has published stories by Ian Rankin, Julian Rathbone, Maureen O'Brien, Steve Rasnic Tem, Martin Edwards ... Two winners of the £1,500 Crime Writers Association Short Story Dagger in just three years of eligibility. Every unagented contributor has received a letter of interest from at least one major London literary agency.

The standard is high, and the Editor is dedicated to keeping it that way. The only advertisements in *Crimewave* are for crime fiction from other publishers.

Andy Cox welcomes submissions of short stories across the entire spectrum of crime fiction, but says, 'We're not looking for cri-fi off the telly – *Crimewave* stories are not clichéd.'

He writes: 'Please study *Crimewave* before submitting, and always enclose appropriate return postage. Overseas submissions should be disposable and accompanied by two International Reply Coupons or an e-mail address (this option is for overseas submissions only). We are unable to reply otherwise.

'Always enclose a covering letter. Manuscripts should be double spaced on A4 paper with good margins all round and preferably mailed flat or folded no more than once.

'There is no length restriction on the stories we publish. No reprints, multiple or simultaneous submissions. Letters and queries are welcome by e-mail but unsolicited submissions are not – they will simply be deleted.'

Contracts are exchanged on acceptance, and payment is made on publication, plus copies.

Crimewave is rapidly becoming a prestigious showcase for crime writers, and is acquiring an international reputation. It merits your very best work.

DOGS MONTHLY

Editor: Ruth Chapman

R.T.C. Associates, Ascot House, High Street, Ascot, Berkshire SL5 7HG.

Tel: 01344 628269. Fax: 01344 622771.

Website: www.dogsmonthly.co.uk

Monthly, £2.95. Founded 1983. Circulation a. Publishes non-fiction and an occasional short story. Pay band A, at the end of the month of publication.

Dogs Monthly is a magazine for dog-enthusiasts, from professional breeders to family pet-owners. It is the longest-established monthly magazine about dogs available to the general public.

Dogs Monthly research shows that its readers 'want more than a *"Hello"* magazine with hints about clipping nails' (quoted from the website). With its core philosophy that dogs are good for people, the magazine has distinct and particular aims which are actively promoted by its Editor, staff and writers, who are all 'dedicated to the welfare of dogs and to wider dog ownership' – see the website for information about *Dogs Monthly*'s readers and the strengths the magazine has built over the years.

A typical issue of *Dogs Monthly* will have 70 to 80 pages, of which just under a third are advertisements – for dog clubs, dog foods, dog insurance policies, dog training ... anything 'doggy'. It also contains, within the advertisements, much information on dog-breeders – a Breeders' Directory.

There are usually several pages of news – new products, dog club activities, competitions – and pages of specialist dog-care advice, including a regular holistic section; there are also 'doggy' book reviews. There is a puzzle page that includes a prize crossword, and there is now a double-page section for younger readers.

Dogs Monthly, acknowledging that many dog owners also keep a pet cat or two, includes one or two features on aspects of the world of cats.

The editorial content – always well-illustrated with either photographs or line drawings – focuses strongly on knowledgeable, authoritative articles about 'the history, background and politics of the world of dogs as pets, workers and competitors'. In one issue we reviewed there were features on 'the intrinsic value of dogs as pets – and as status symbols' (written by a regular columnist); the Bergamasco mini-breed; police dogs in Texas; a 'Crufts Special'; the artist Cecil Aldin; the Basenji 'Silent Hunters of Africa'; and Ingrid Melis's sanctuary at Benalmadena Pueblo on the Costa Del Sol.

You really need to know your subject to write for *Dogs Monthly*, but if you're a knowledgeable dog-owning freelance who can supply appropriate illustrations, the Editor would be happy to consider your work. You can either send an idea with a synopsis showing how you plan to handle your topic, or a finished article on spec. Decisions usually come in about a month.

There is also an occasional opportunity for an 800-word short-short (non-shaggy) dog story 'of real quality'.

Tip: Do look at the website – there's a wealth of information there, including an archive list of breeds giving the years when they were featured in the magazine.

ESSENTIALLY AMERICA

For the independent traveller

Editorial Director: Mary Moore Mason

Editorial Office: 55 Hereford Road, London W2 5BB.

Tel: 020 7243 6954. E-mail: marymooremason@phoenixip.com

Every two months, £2.95. Founded 1994. Circulation a. Publishes non-fiction only. *No short stories or poetry*. Pay band D, at the end of the month of publication.

Essentially America is published in the UK by Phoenix International Publishing, Hadlow House, Hadlow Down, East Sussex TN22 4EP. The magazine aims to promote North American travel and lifestyle for a British readership, for the interest of everyone in the UK and Ireland who enjoys reading about and/or travelling in the USA and Canada.

A typical issue will have 68 perfect-bound, colourfully illustrated pages. Of these, about 9 or 10 will be advertisements, mainly, as you would expect, for attractions, travel destinations and accommodation. There are also a number of bound-in or poly-bagged advertising-supported supplements throughout the year

Editorially, there are sections on travel news, 'showbiz', websites to visit, book reviews, restaurants, a prize crossword, and a Letters page – in one issue we reviewed this consisted of three queries about travelling to and within North America, with helpful answers which included useful sources of information.

Essentially America publishes articles on a wide variety of US and Canadian subjects: people, places, history, cuisine and lifestyle. In this issue, there were seven general features, including: 'On tour with the TV series ... the favourite locations of *Seinfeld, Sex and the City* and *The Sopranos*'; 'Las Vegas's fabulous fantasy hotels'; 'Space men and star gazers ... view the night sky through a giant telescope, visit one of the famous *Apollo* space modules and even have lunch with a spaceman'; 'Elvis – 25 years on'; 'On site with *The Shipping News* – on location in Newfoundland with Kevin Spacey, Kate Blanchett and Dame Judi Dench'; and 'American icons ... in the footsteps of the immigrants to the Statue of Liberty, Ellis Island and the Lower East Side Tenement Museum'.

There were also four travel features: 'Pennsylvania' ... home to the Declaration of Independence and the Gettysburg Address, the Allegheny National Forest, America's favourite chocolate bar, Amish and Mennonite communities, and an Andy Warhol museum; 'North America's most beautiful gardens – from the Deep South to Québec Province'; 'Tapping into Tucson' ... Arizona's Sonoran Desert and the legendary Tombstone; and 'Star City: Nashville, Music City USA' – home to the fabulous new Country Music Hall of Fame and of the Grand Ole Opry.

Features are packed with facts and tips for greater enjoyment of holidays, touring and so on, and should be supplemented by sidebars giving travel information.

All the articles are profusely illustrated in colour. If you can offer quality pictures with your feature, your chances will be considerably enhanced. Photos illustrating lifestyles are as welcome as views and landmarks. *Essentially America* accepts most formats, including digital.

Approach with ideas in the first instance. Length will be discussed if they're interested in what you offer.

Tip: The writing is energetic and authoritative as well as being highly readable.

ESSENTIALS

Editor: Karen Livermore

Editor's PA: Gillian Bullock

Room 569, King's Reach Tower, Stamford Street, London SE1 9LS.

Tel: 020 7261 6970. Fax: 020 7261 5262. E-mail: essentials@ipcmedia.com

Monthly, £2.20. Founded 1988. Circulation c. Publishes non-fiction only – *don't send short stories or poetry*. Pay band D, made at the end of the month of publication.

Essentials is a glossy magazine aimed at women in their late twenties and over, almost certainly in some form of stable relationship, probably with primary-school-age children – and a keen family/home-maker. The typical reader may well juggle job (maybe part-time) and family – and while enthusiastic about making things herself she doesn't always have much time. *Essentials* covers a wide range of topics, with the emphasis firmly on practical matters.

A typical issue of *Essentials* will have about 140 perfect-bound pages (plus a bound-in paper dressmaking pattern). About a third of the pages will be filled with a wide range of advertisements – from beauty and food products to car insurance, from laundry aids to home study courses. Included in the adverts are several pages offering a range of services from cosmetic surgery through maternity clothes to telephone chat-lines.

On the editorial side, there are several regular sections: fashion, health and beauty, parenting, home-making (from DIY to refurnishing), 'work & money', travel and cooking. Each month, there's a 32-page pull-out '*Essentials* ideas' section, hole-punched ready for filing and packed with home-making, cookery (one issue we read included 'The ultimate guide to mushrooms') and dressmaking ideas. There's an astrology column, a couple of 'agony' columns, reader offers, and a page of 'treats of the month' offering desirable freebies like a weekend break in Europe and DVD players. The Letters page uses four or five 50- to 100-word mostly back-issue-related letters each month. The star letter wins a valuable prize, for example two dozen bottles of New Zealand wine, the others receive £20.

There are not all that many opportunities for the 'ordinary' freelance to contribute one-off features to *Essentials* – they have staff feature writers, and celebrity columnists – but there are some: *Essentials* pays £100 for every 'Real Women, Real Lives' story they print, so if something important has happened to you they might be interested. One inspirational story we read was about a woman who saved the life of a neighbour who was shot, and who faced her own death from cancer with courage and fortitude; the story was told by the woman's son, and included a sidebar with information on first aid training. In the same issue there was a 'Reader home' feature showing how a children's book illustrator 'gets creative at home'.

If you have a *really* relevant idea for an *Essentials* feature, send the editor a BRIEF outline. (Maximum length for finished features is 2,000 words.)

EVE

The smarter woman's read

Editor: Jane Bruton

Features Director: Victoria Woodhall

BBC Worldwide Ltd, AG200, 80 Wood Lane, London W12 0TT.

Tel: 020 8433 3767. Fax: 020 8433 3359.

E-mail: eve@bbc.co.uk

Website: www.allabouteve.co.uk

Monthly, £2.80. Founded 2000. Circulation c. Publishes non-fiction only. Query essential. *No fiction or poetry*. Pay band D, at the end of the month of publication.

Eve is a high quality glossy magazine a distinct cut above the average women's title. It's intelligent, contemporary, glamorous but not 'flashy', practical but never dull. *Eve* was also the first women's magazine to launch in tandem with an interactive website.

A typical issue of *Eve* will have about 200 pages of which about 25% will be advertisements, for cars, clothes and accessories, beauty products, fragrances, pharmaceutical products, food, and other BBC Worldwide magazines. The ads reflect the interests and aspirations of the magazine's target reader, who is described on the website as 'open-minded, bright, positive, worldly, grown-up, realistic, demanding, discerning and funny', whatever her age.

Editorially, *Eve* has everything you would expect to find in a women's magazine: fashion (thoughtfully balanced to suit every budget), health and beauty, home-making, food and wine, travel, finance, reviews, horoscopes and an 'agony' column. There's a section headed 'How to do everything better', a serendipitous collection of advice: in two issues we read, this section included how to ... have a better financial relationship ... get him in the mood with food ... be a happy camper ... get your home on TV ... fight off a shark ... re-ignite passion ... shop abroad ... run a marathon ... know your wine ... write well ... co-habit ... save the world – a nutshell illustration of *Eve*'s scope.

There are plenty of famous names here, too: Kevin Spacey, Dervla Kirwan, George Alaghia, Meg Ryan, Katherine Hamnett, Rosie Millard, Sheryl Crow, Helen Lederer – all these appeared in these issues.

Every issue of *Eve* is packed with features, too, on an incredibly wide range of topics. Here are a random few to give you a taste: 'Want to be an aristocrat? All you need is a little cash and a lot of nerve', 'Handling terrorism – the new self-defence', 'Flights of fantasy – What ever happened to trips to the moon?', 'Now hear this – Why men are insulting you in advertising', 'Sex bombshell – Jaw-dropping news about who's really male or female', 'It was just not my day for dying – The stewardess who survived a mid-air terrorist bombing', 'The two faces of addiction – When a man is alcoholic, there's another side to the story: his wife's', and 'Can rock gods paint? How art critics rate works by Bowie, McCartney and others'.

Eve is a feast of meaty reading. Give yourself plenty of time to study several issues and absorb the style. *Eve* is definitely different. If you think you can offer a feature of the required quality and originality, send an outline *in writing* to the Features Director, together with cuttings of published work – *Eve* is not a market for beginners. Length will be discussed if they're interested.

Tip: Features in *Eve* are thoroughly researched and exceptionally well written.

FAMILY CIRCLE

Editor: Julie Barton Breck (020 7261 6195)

Editor's PA: Susan Kirkhouse (020 7261 6195)

Features Editor: Emma Burstall (020 7261 5957)

IPC Media, King's Reach Tower, Stamford Street, London SE1 9LS.

Website: www.ipcmedia.co.uk

Monthly, £1.75. Founded 1964. Circulation c. Non-fiction only. Query essential. *Don't send short stories*. Pay band D, at the end of the month of publication.

Family Circle is a bright, cheerful monthly magazine publishing a wide variety of features. Its target readership is mainly family-based women of 35-plus, often with a part-time job and children at school.

A typical issue of *Family Circle* will have about 100 highly illustrated saddle-stitched pages of which about a quarter will be advertisements, for foodstuffs, pharmaceutical products, cosmetics, household equipment etc. There will be a number of special reader offers, for the likes of cleaning equipment, clothing, cutlery, miniature trees, plus reader competitions offering substantial prizes like cars and four-figure money; there will also be a selection of 'giveaways', and an occasional free gift offered to every reader.

Editorially, there are several regular sections: home-making and personal lifestyle, health, beauty, fashion, cookery and gardening. There are usually a dozen or so pages of fashion carefully chosen to be relevant to the readership. There's a prize cross-word, a 'Stars' page, a travel section; the Letters page, 'Have your say', uses 6 or 7 letters (100 words, about half back-issue-related) each month, giving a bottle of champagne worth £18.99 for each one printed, with the best letter winning a luxury hamper.

The magazine does not accept any unsolicited articles or short stories.

In the masthead they state: 'We are rarely able to use unsolicited manuscripts and readers should keep their own copies. Payment for use of such material is at the editor's discretion. Please don't send valuable mss or pictures – we do our best to return them safely if stamps are enclosed but cannot guarantee this.'

Nevertheless, while some *Family Circle* features in the issue we reviewed were undoubtedly staff-written, others could have been produced by experienced free-lance writers. Typical of *potential* freelance material were: 'Too close for comfort?', on living near the in-laws; the diary of a couple who built their own house; and 'From the heart', a letter from a wife to her husband in appreciation of his saving her life by giving her one of his kidneys. Interviews with appropriate celebrities would probably have an excellent chance.

If you think you have an idea for a *relevant* feature for *Family Circle*, contact the Features Department with a *brief* outline plus, if possible, one or two cuttings or photocopies of similar published work, and hope for editorial interest.

THE FIELD

Editor: Jonathan Young

Editor's PA: Marcella Bingley

King's Reach Tower, Stamford Street, London SE1 9LS.

Tel: 020 7261 5198. Fax: 020 7261 5358.

E-mail: marcella_bingley@ipcmedia.com

Website: www.thefield.co.uk

Monthly, £3.30. Founded 1853. Circulation a. Non-fiction only. *Do not send short stories or poetry.* Pay band D, at the end of the month of publication.

The Field is a glossy, well-illustrated monthly magazine from IPC. Founded as a weekly paper for gentlemen, it has changed its frequency but not its target readership. This is largely, but not exclusively, male – and undoubtedly affluent. It caters for the real country-person rather than those with a sentimental fondness for the *idea* of the country. Field sports and rural and environmental concerns have always been central to its interests, and most other 'gentlemen's activities' are also covered.

A typical issue of *The Field* will have 126 or so much-illustrated pages of which about a third are advertisements – for country properties, guns and gun accessories, fly-fishing accessories, outdoor clothes, country-house furniture, jewellery and antiques.

On the editorial side, there are many regular sections/pages, covering property, country courses, cookery, motoring, art and antiques, wine, country events, country queries, bridge – and a prize crossword.

There are plenty of one-off features too – and the editor welcomes the opportunity to consider really *Field-relevant* feature ideas. Something out of the ordinary, yet within the magazine's areas of interest, would be the best bet. But submit only *brief* article outlines, in writing, and only if you have the appropriate expertise. Illustrations are usually commissioned – but complete 'packages' of (expert) words and (top quality) pictures are always welcomed. You might try phoning (be brief and business-like) or e-mailing after a couple of weeks to enquire about interest in the outline.

One-off features (anything from 800 to 2,000 words long) in *The Field* have included illustrated articles about clumber spaniels; a shooting party at Balfour Castle, Shapinsay; a feature on photographer Valentine Atkinson; the increase in sightings of sharks and other exotic creatures around our coasts; and an interview with Vinnie Jones, 'the hard man of football, film, fishing and the shooting field'. A broad 'field' of interests.

There is also a regular section in *The Field* called 'Out in the Field' that includes comments on current concerns, and previews forthcoming country events, exhibitions, etc., with date-relevant snippets. In the issue we reviewed, for example, there were reports (ranging from 100 to 300 words) on improving Salisbury Plain as a wildlife site; Buffalo Blue cheese; a deep-sea port threat to salmon; and saving lapwings on a Nottinghamshire farm. Such snippets are often freelance contributed (and bylined). A good opening if you can produce what they want.

FOCUS

Editor: Emma Bayley

Origin Publishing Ltd, 14th Floor, Tower House, Fairfax Street, Bristol BS1 3BN.

Tel: 0117 927 9009. Fax: 0117 934 9008.

E-mail: emmabayley@originpublishing.co.uk Website: www.focusmag.co.uk

Monthly, £2.95. Founded 1996. Circulation b. Publishes non-fiction only (news, photo-essays, photo-journalism). *Don't send short stories or poetry.* Pay band D, on publication.

Focus is a magazine about the world around us, covering popular science, technology, medicine, culture, nature, wildlife and the environment. Its target readership is mainly young upmarket men, but its wide-ranging content offers much of interest to all ages and both sexes.

A typical issue of *Focus* has 108 colourfully and profusely illustrated saddle-stitched pages of which 8 or 9 carry advertisements, for a range of products and services as varied as the magazine's content – PCs and printers, mobile phones, watches, kites, paragliding and hot-air ballooning, financial services, books and exhibitions.

Editorially, each issue of *Focus* has several regular columns: 'Q&As', questions and answers on topics like, for example: 'How effective are silencers on guns?', 'How long is "once in a blue moon"?', 'How does the non-stick layer stick to frying pans?'. There's a multiple-choice quiz (with answers), a 'Quick chat with ...' the likes of Roger Needham, director of Microsoft's Cambridge research lab, Tony Wheeler, founder of Lonely Planet, and survival expert Ray Mears. There's also a prize cross-word in every issue.

There's a news section, 'Agenda', using reports on everything from archaeology to space, from evolution to insulation – 50 to 200 words, most with pix.

Every issue of *Focus* has a dozen complete features covering a carefully balanced variety of topics. In the two issues we reviewed, topics included (to give you just a few examples): the reconstruction of the great library of Alexandria, destroyed over 2,000 years ago; 'On the trail of Dracula', in search of the real story and the people behind the legend; an investigation into the effectiveness of glass, paper and plastics recycling in the UK; 'MMR: the lost science'; how the economic theories of Karl Marx influenced the 20th century; 'Raising the Kursk'; 'Unearthing a Roman with the Time Team'; 'What's behind obesity?'; how new natural history filming techniques are helping scientists to analyse animal movement ...

The writing is top quality - intelligent, accessible and authoritative. The Editor will consider relevant ideas with synopses, in writing. Features are usually between 750 and 2,500 words, but length will be discussed if they like what you offer.

Focus is known for its stunning award-winning photography – its content is about 50 per cent photographic. Most features open on a double-page spread and are sup-ported by several further photos and/or colour illustrations. Colour only is used, nearly always transparencies, the bigger the format the better – and always absolutely pin-sharp. Obviously, if you can offer excellent photos or illustrations you'll increase your chances of success. The Editor is particularly interested in quality photo-essays.

Tip: Don't even think about offering anything before you've studied several issues thoroughly – analyse and absorb the style of both text and pictures.

GEOGRAPHICAL

The Royal Geographical Society Magazine

Editor: Carolyn Fry

Deputy Editor: Jo Bourne

Unit 11, 124-128 Barlby Road, London WI0 6BL.

Tel: 020 8960 6400. Fax: 020 8960 6004.

E-mail: magazine@geographical.co.uk   Website: www.geographical.co.uk

Monthly, £3.25. Founded 1935. Circulation a. Non-fiction only. Query essential. *No short stories or poetry.* Pay band D, at the end of the month of publication.

The magazine of the Royal Geographical Society, *Geographical* is targeted at members (Fellows) of the Society but is clearly of interest to many 'lay' readers and is readily available from larger newsagents. *Geographical* is published by Campion Interactive Publishing, on behalf of the Royal Geographical Society.

Each issue of *Geographical* has about 100 colourful glossy perfect-bound pages of which 20 or so will be advertisements. The adverts reflect the readership, offering outdoor clothing and boots, binoculars, mobile phones and other essential items of travellers' equipment, appeals from conservation and other charitable societies, plus expeditions and travel accommodation.

Editorially, there are a number of regular sections/features: ethical finance, motors and travel, geographical news and views from around the world, reviews of relevant products, news of what's going to be on in the month ahead, a prize crossword and competitions (including their prestigious 'Photographer of the Year' contest).

There is a mostly back-issue-related Letters page using 7 or 8 longish letters per issue, the prize letter winning a £75 voucher (for Amazon.co.uk, the online book, CD and video retailer), and a page of interesting questions and readers' answers, using 3 or 4 per issue.

Each issue of *Geographical* also has maybe 7 or 8 one-off feature articles on a range of topics such as environment, exploration, history, archaeology and travel. Many of these are contributed by well-known explorers or academics in the geographical field, or are written in-house, but two or three features in each issue are usually by experienced freelance writers. In the two issues we reviewed, such one-offs included a journey to Istanbul on the Orient Express (with a selection of the world's greatest train journeys); gambling mania among Taiwan's pigeon fanciers; how an inheritance of old letters revealed the experiences of two brothers who emigrated to Australia in 1839; the discovery of a labyrinth of caverns and tunnels under Liverpool which were built by the eccentric tycoon Joseph Williamson; an eight-week road journey from Chile to Brazil made by a couple with their five children; and an interview with wildlife campaigner and documentary-maker Valmik Thapar about his lifelong passion for tigers and his concern for their future.

All the features in *Geographical* are lavishly illustrated in colour, sometimes by the writers, sometimes not.

If you have detailed geographical knowledge or recent experience of a specific area and can formulate this as a *relevant* feature idea - it would be worth submitting a detailed outline to the Editor. Don't waste time with ideas for travel articles without geographical content, though. Be warned – it's got to be really good to get a go-ahead.

GIRL TALK

Where girls get together

Editor: Claire Funge

Room A1130, BBC Woodlands, 80 Wood Lane, London W12 0TT.

Tel: 020 8576 3543. E-mail: girltalk.magazine@bbc.co.uk

Every two weeks, £1.10. Circulation b. Short stories, serial photo-stories, puzzles, quizzes, craft and simple cookery. Pay band C, on publication.

Girl Talk is a lively, colourful magazine for girls aged 7 to 12. A typical issue will have 32 pages of which about four will be advertisements carefully targeting the magazine's young readers: dolls, computer games, snacks and sweets, animal charities, and other BBC publications. There are occasional 'bumper' issues of 48 pages with a dozen or so pages of adverts. There's usually a cover-mount, a purse, a pen, pretty hairgrips or the like.

Every issue has several poster pictures, of young pop stars and appealing animals. There are always pages of fashion and the kind of 'stuff' that girls love like accessories, jewellery and toiletries, plus 'What's Hot': news and chat about young pop groups and personalities, and reviews of videos, TV programmes, singles and books.

Girl Talk has a regular 'Paws 'n' Claws' section by vet Emma, one of the stars of BBC TV's *Vet School* and *Vets in Practice*. There are puzzles, quizzes, reader offers, and fun features like 'Potty Pastimes' and 'Mates Makeover', things to make (and bake), interviews with young pop stars, horoscopes by fluffy feline forecaster 'Mystic Biscuit', and letters from *Girl Talk*'s young readers, with a prize for the Star letter.

There's a *Girl Talk* Club, with a Lucky Numbers prize every week.

Girl Talk has a short story in every issue, length no more than 550 words, using contemporary themes and language, and always featuring a girl of the target readership age as the main protagonist. One story we read told how Sarah danced to success in spite of losing her pink ballet shoes, another centred on an argument over a skateboard between Alice and her little brother. Stories are often tied in with events and/or times of the year.

The Editor is happy to receive synopses as well as complete mss. Stories must be original and unpublished - *Girl Talk* buys them on an 'All rights' basis.

Girl Talk also has one photo-script and one picture-script serial in every issue. The photo-script serial we saw was about four 'Best Friends', and the picture-script featured a 'Girl Band'. These stories are told entirely through dialogue. The first part of 'Best Friends' opened with a 10-word introductory caption but no closing caption, 'Girl Band' had a 10-word introductory caption and a 24-word closing caption trailing the next episode. (There were no other captions.) Episodes had 11 or 12 frames each. (See 'Writing Picture-Story Scripts', page 138.)

If you have an idea for a serial send a synopsis and scripts for two or three sample episodes, and you might be lucky enough to have your serial featured in *Girl Talk*.

GOOD HOUSEKEEPING

For the grown-up woman

Editor-in-Chief: Lindsay Nicholson

Personal Assistant: Tanya Penney - Tel: 020 7439 5072

Features Editor: Kerry Fowler

National Magazine Company, National Magazine House, 72 Broadwick Street, London WIV 2BP.

Monthly, £2.70. Founded 1922. Circulation d. Publishes non-fiction. *Query essential.* Occasionally publishes fiction, but *only* from commissioned 'name' writers or from competition winners, so *don't submit short stories.* Pay band D, at the end of the month of publication.

Good Housekeeping is still in the forefront of quality magazines for women. It is well aimed at the relatively affluent woman in her late thirties and over, whose interests lie close to home and family life although, nowadays, she might also have a career.

A typical issue of *Good Housekeeping* will have about 186 glossy, perfect-bound pages of which about half will usually be advertisements. The display adverts are for clothes, cosmetics, furnishings, kitchen equipment, food etc. There are about a dozen pages of classified ads, too, for everything from cookery courses and cosmetic surgery to holiday accommodation and sofas.

Editorially, *Good Housekeeping* has a number of regular multi-page sections or departments, mostly staff-written: homes and gardens, health, fashion and beauty, and travel. There are a couple of comment columns (one from Maureen Lipman) - plus the predictable astrology page, reviews and a Letters page. (Write to 'Letters to the Editor' - there are about half a dozen letters each month, from 40 to 150 words, almost all back-issue related; at the time of writing, each letter printed received flowers to the value of £25, with a £40 bouquet for the Star letter.) There are always reader offers and a prize crossword and, of course, in each issue there are the 'Good Housekeeping Institute' pages, packed with succulent Institute-tested recipes and helpful consumer reports.

There are also half-a-dozen or so one-off feature articles in each issue, clearly written by freelance writers, some with well-known names. In the issues we reviewed, articles we assessed to be freelance-written (many under the banner heading 'Real Life Issues') included the story of how a disabled skier inspires others to have 'the confidence to go for it'; a plea for home-making skills to be given the recognition they deserve through a change of image and title: 'Call me what you like but don't call me *that'* – 'that' being 'just a housewife'. And there were the stories of three women who changed their lives, one by becoming a Muslim after a Church of England upbringing; the second by moving from angry ultra-left-wing radicalism ('I suppose the next step would have been political violence') to joining a major world peace movement and working as a naturopath trained in conflict and peace management; and the third by halving her weight and becoming a marathon runner. These articles were between 700 and 1,600 words long.

If you have an idea for a suitable feature for *Good Housekeeping* - human interest, health, personal growth/improvement, personality profiles - send in a *brief* well-thought-through outline/query. Then await the response - within 2 to 3 weeks. You could get a (possibly non-committal) go ahead.

The Magazine Writer's Handbook

HOME & COUNTRY

The National Voice of The Women's Institutes

Editor: Susan Seager

Practicals Editor: Clare Royals

Features Editor: Sheila Purcell

NFWI, 104 New King's Road, London SW6 4LY.

Tel: 020 7731 5777. Fax: 020 7736 4061.

E-mail: h&ced@nfwi.org.uk   NFWI Website: www.womens-institute.org.uk

Monthly, £1.10 (£.1.15 from January 2003). (Subscription only; for details call the Subscription Department on 020 7371 9300.) Founded 1919. Circulation b. Non-fiction and occasional short stories. Query advisable. *Don't send poetry.* Pay band C, at the end of the month of publication.

The official journal of the National Federation of Women's Institutes, *Home & Country* is available on subscription. Outside contributions (including *relevant* material from men) are welcomed. The magazine's core readership is obvious: WI members - relatively affluent, largely middle-aged women with broadly country/rural lives and/or interests.

A typical issue of *Home & Country* will have about 68 colourful (but not brash) saddle-stitched pages of which roughly one third will be advertisements - 50:50 display and classifieds. The display adverts are fairly typical of a monthly magazine aimed at this age group; the classifieds are mainly for B&B accommodation - from Land's End to ...

Editorially, the magazine includes, of course, about a dozen pages of WI news, features and 'business'. There are regular sections dealing with food and cooking, gardening, health, book reviews and travel.

There are usually a few pages of craft instruction. In one issue we reviewed there were detailed instructions on how to make a decorative shelf unit to display a prized collection. If you have ideas for this spot, contact the Practicals Editor.

There is a lively Letters page using 9 or 10 often back-issue- and WI-related letters, about 40 to 150 words each, with a prize for the best.

As well as the regular features, there are several one-off articles, some - but by no means all - from WI members. Subjects range from rural and environment issues to travel and hobbies. One issue we read included a lively debate, under the heading 'Taking sides', giving two opposing views, 'For' and 'Against', on the question 'Should smacking children be banned?' The same issue included a feature titled 'Industrial revelation' in which the writer enjoyed 'a journey back in time' through Shropshire, visiting the Raven Hotel and the 700-year-old market at Much Wenlock, the cast iron bridge at Ironbridge, the RAF museum at Cosford and the Roman Ruins of Wroxeter City and Baths, among other tourist attractions. Another article told of a journey on the North Yorkshire Moors Railway to Goathland station, scene of filming for the TV series *Heartbeat* and, transformed into 'Hogsmeade', the film *Harry Potter and the Philosopher's Stone.*

Articles should not exceed 1,000 words and where appropriate there is a fact-packed sidebar. Illustrations will always be welcome but clearly some are agency-provided. It's essential to query feature ideas before submitting - to confirm interest.

HOMES & GARDENS

Editor: Isobel McKenzie-Price

Personal Assistant: Caroline Norton (Tel: 020 7261 5678)

Features Editor: Katherine Sorrell (Tel: 020 7261 6181)

IPC Magazines Ltd, King's Reach Tower, Stamford Street, London SE1 9LS.

Monthly, £3.00. Founded 1919. Circulation c. Non-fiction only. *Don't send short stories or poetry.* Pay band D, at the end of the month of publication.

Homes & Gardens is stylish, upmarket, and targeted mainly - but not solely - at women who are (or aspire to be) artistically house-and-garden-proud, sophisticated and affluent, probably aged from around 35 up.

A typical issue of *Homes & Gardens* will have about 186 glossy perfect-bound pages, plus, in the London editions only, a bound-in 24-page supplement (mainly advertisements) detailing what's available in the capital's shops. Of the magazine itself, about forty per cent of the pages will be advertisements - for furniture, carpets and soft furnishings, household equipment and fittings, cars, garden furniture ... and some food items. Occasionally there are bound-in advertising sections, often for specialist stores and services, and banded supplements focused on, for example, conservatories, decorating and so on. There are often special offers - luxurious soft furnishings, occasional tables and the like - and desirable treats and giveaways like a stainless steel double oven and hob, a luxury weekend at Claridge's, toile de jouy bedspreads, all these in one issue we reviewed.

Editorially, the pages are lavishly but always tastefully illustrated. Regular sections/departments deal with houses, gardens, decorating and cooking. There are book reviews, shopping on the internet, answers to decorating queries, things to make and do ... There are always several pages of news of current and upcoming events and exhibitions, too.

Clearly, most of the one-off articles in each issue of *Homes & Gardens* are staff-generated commissioned features: for most of those about house interiors, the rooms are 'styled' before being professionally photographed. But there are usually potential opportunities for freelance writer-initiated features too. One issue we saw included: a short feature on how 'your postcode can have a direct - and undesirable - effect on your love life' (about 700 words); the timeless appeal of celadon, a ceramic that's been around for three thousand years (about 1,000 words); and a profusely illustrated feature on the home and life of the Temple family of Donegal, producers of beautiful hand-woven tweeds (about 700 words). The latter two features are typical of the *Homes & Gardens* style: a feast of beautiful photographs accompanied by concise, informative writing.

If you have a really interesting and *relevant* feature idea that is suitable for *Homes & Gardens* - submit a *brief* written outline, and enclose illustrative snapshots where appropriate. You could get a go-ahead.

Tip: Don't send unsolicited finished manuscripts - these are not welcome.

IDEAL HOME

Britain's best-selling decorating magazine

Editor: Jane Parbury

Editor's PA: Caroline Norton

IPC Media Ltd, King's Reach Tower, Stamford Street, London SE1 9LS.

Tel: 020 7261 6474. Fax: 020 7261 6697.

E-mail: ideal_home@ipcmedia.com   Website: www.ipcmedia.com

Monthly, £2.60. Founded 1920. Circulation c. Non-fiction only. *Query preferred.* Pay band D, at the end of the month of publication.

Ideal Home is another of IPC's quality magazines. Despite the ever-increasing competition in 'home' magazines, *Ideal Home* is as fresh and up-to-date today as when it was launched more than 80 years ago, and remains one of our leading home-interest publications. Its readership is undoubtedly affluent, fashionably house-proud, likes to keep up with the trends, and is predominantly female and probably in the 25-45 age group. The magazine offers a well-balanced combination of aspiration and practicality, inviting readers to 'keep your finger on the pulse of new ideas'.

A typical issue of *Ideal Home* will have around 240 perfect-bound pages, much illustrated and always colourful but never brash. Many issues come with an additional supplement, too - the issue we reviewed had a separate 52-page booklet titled 'Be Your Own Interior Designer'.

There will be many advertisements covering a wide range of home equipment and furnishings: bedding, kitchens, bathrooms, furniture, soft furnishings and home accessories - both trendy and traditional. There will also be 9 or 10 pages of classified ads, a 'Shopping Directory', offering a variety of temptations for the house and garden ranging from hand-forged iron beds to interior design courses.

Ideal Home's editorial pages are full of lavishly illustrated features about lovely homes and gardens, always supported by practical information on how to achieve the look and what it will cost. There are advice articles on home maintenance, decorating and cooking, and practical problem-solving on the home front, 'Buyer's Guides' to a range of household equipment, and several 'Buy the best' guides.

There is a Letters page, 'From you to us', using around half-a-dozen mainly back-issue-related contributions of 60 words or less, with a prize for the Star letter - in the issue we reviewed the prize was an Indesit dishwasher worth £350.

The same issue had a feature giving detailed advice on how to avoid decorating disasters; another showed imaginative ways to display pictures in the home, and there was one on 'Clever tricks for cleaning'. Other features showed '34 ways to update your kitchen', and '5 fantastic looks for bathrooms'. The same issue featured 5 real readers' homes and lifestyles, with 'Style Files' showing how to get the look.

There is little scope for the non-specialist offering; most main features are staff-written or specially commissioned. There are usually one or two features that *could* be provided by a competent freelance; these appear to lie mainly in the 'real homes' section - there are five or six of these features in each issue - but the Editor will consider articles on all aspects of home-making and decorating. She is willing to consider full manuscripts on spec - but you'd be much wiser to write in first with a query/outline. No fiction, of course.

Not a big market, but a good one to be seen in.

INTERZONE

Editor: David Pringle

217 Preston Drove, Brighton, East Sussex BN1 6FL.

Tel: 01273 504710. E-mail: interzone@cix.co.uk

Website: www.sfsite.com/interzone

Monthly, £3.00. Founded 1982. Circulation a. Publishes science fiction/fantasy short stories plus features and interviews relevant to the genre. Pay band A, at the end of the month of publication.

Interzone is a stylishly produced, well-illustrated, professional yet totally independent publication: it receives just a small Arts Council grant. In the world of science fiction, it is internationally renowned; it is the only British magazine to have won the prestigious Hugo award.

Interzone's readers are science fiction/fantasy fans. It is a specialist-interest fiction/ fiction-related magazine at the 'cutting edge'. It's not a magazine to offer 'any old weirdo story' to; its requirements are specific and its style needs to be studied. (It's way past Robert Heinlein and Anne McCaffrey yet not into the stranger realms of some SF small-press magazines.) It's essential to read several issues before submitting anything - or you'll be wasting everybody's time. (Information about back issues is in the magazine, which you can buy from major booksellers as well as newsagents.)

A typical issue of *Interzone* will have 68 pages of which only two or three will be advertisements, including a page of small ads. Editorially, there are several regular columns/sections: film and TV reviews, several pages of in-depth book reviews (one issue we read had eight pages with more than a dozen reviews) plus four or five pages listing 'Books received' (over 70 books mentioned) giving publication dates and brief summaries of their content, an author interview and an SF-world gossip column. The Editor - who has an encyclopaedic knowledge of SF - occasionally allows himself to offer his views in a lengthy editorial: alternatively the space is given over to readers' letters. And then there is the fiction. There are six or seven SF or fantasy stories in most issues; *Interzone* has published such luminaries as Brian Aldiss, Iain Banks, Michael Moorcroft and Lisa Tuttle among many others, but the Editor is always on the lookout for new talent.

In his guidelines, the Editor says 'We are looking for innovative, entertaining, well written and up-to-date science fiction and fantasy. We are unlikely to accept hackneyed space opera, sword-and-sorcery tales, or traditional ghost stories.'

Submitted stories should be within the range 2,000 to 6,000 words (mark the wordage on the cover sheet); send only one story at a time; get the layout right - paragraphs indented, no line space between paragraphs, good wide margins and no 'dotty' typescript. Don't staple the pages, use a paperclip; don't use padded bags, cardboard folders or anything that hinders postal delivery and increases postal costs. As well as the essential ms-sized s.a.e., send a stamped addressed postcard if you would like acknowledgement of receipt. *Interzone* buys First English-Language Rights (i.e., including American). Decisions take *at least* two months.

Tip: You can find detailed submission guidelines at the website.

IRELAND'S OWN

Ireland's favourite family magazine for 100 years

Editor: Phil Murphy. Weekly Editions Editor: Sean Nolan.

Channing House, Rowe Street, Wexford, Dublin, Republic of Ireland.

Tel: 00 353 534 0100.

Weekly, 65p (euro .83). Special double issues every month, on seasonal themes: Easter, Christmas, St Patrick's Day, Hallowe'en etc., £1.25 (euro 1.59). Founded 1902. Circulation b. Publishes non-fiction, short fiction and serial stories. Pay band A/B, on publication.

Ireland's Own has been published continuously for 100 years. It's a warm and wholesome family magazine with a readership of all ages. A typical weekly issue will have 40 saddle-stitched pages, illustrated in colour and black-and-white with photographs, line art and cartoons. The monthly issues contain 72 pages. *Ireland's Own* carries very little advertising.

The magazine's content is wonderfully varied. There are articles, article series, short stories, a serial, several regular columns (from established contributors) including 'Stranger than fiction' - ghosts, extra-terrestrials et al - and a crime puzzle story, 'Catch the criminal', with the solution given later in the magazine. There are two 'Singalong' pages, printing the words of 'more of your favourite songs' – typically standards like *The Last Waltz* and *Downtown*, and traditional songs like *Westering Home* and *The Green Hills of Antrim*. There are two pages of letters, many asking for help in finding particular books, records, poetry and song lyrics, or seeking information about family names and contacts - no payment or prizes. There's a page of jokes, paying £5 for the best jokes published each week, and a Pen Friends page.

Every issue has an 8-page children's section, 'Owen's Club', with jokes, puzzles, a cartoon strip, photos of club members' pets, odd facts, a colouring page and an 800-word story - we read about 'George the Dragon' and how Buster the cat went fishing.

Of most interest to the freelance writer are the 7 or 8 feature articles published in every issue. Topics vary widely, and are not necessarily Irish, though of course many are. In one issue we read, there were features on: 'William Lever - the man who brought "sunlight" into millions of homes'; the last execution in Armagh Gaol'; 'A Model Enterprise - Madame Tussaud's'; 'Oscar Bravo' - fifty years of the Oscars; 'The Killing of James Carey'; 'Fastnet Rock Lighthouse - A beacon of hope' and 'St Dubhach's Pilgrimage'. Truly something of interest to everyone!

Length required for articles is 800 to 900 words. Photos should be clear sharp prints.

Ireland's Own has a 'Memories Section' in each issue - a 700-word personal memory, often tinged with nostalgia. The magazine also uses batches of interesting snippets under umbrella titles like 'How Did They Do That?' and 'Did You Know'.

We saw, too, a report on a study by phone makers Motorola comparing phone users to bird types (6 paragraphs of 30-65 words) written by an English freelance we know.

There are two short stories in every issue. 2,000 to 2,500 words; these are traditional, non-experimental, and should have an Irish connection - setting and/or characters.

You need to send a self-addressed envelope plus IRCs - UK stamps are not valid in the Republic. Tell the Editor if your ms is disposable, in which case a business-size envelope and one IRC will do. You'll get a reply within two or three weeks.

JUNIOR

The world's finest parenting magazine

Publisher and Editor-in-Chief: Chris Taggart

Editor: Catherine O'Dolan

Features Editor: Hannah Jolliffe

Beach Magazines and Publishing, 4 Cromwell Place, London SW7 2JE.

Tel: 020 7761 8900. Fax: 020 7761 8901. E-mail: editorial@juniormagazine.co.uk

Monthly (11 issues a year), £2.90. Founded 1998. Circulation b. Non-fiction only. Query advisable. *Don't send short stories or poetry.* Pay band D, on publication.

Junior targets intelligent and probably pretty affluent parents of children aged from birth to about eight years of age, and those aspiring to such a lifestyle - a different type of reader from those who read the more conventional parenting magazines. The content is emphatically upmarket, the clothes and equipment featured being distinctly Harrods/Harvey Nichols, not M&S/Matalan.

Junior is glossy but far from superficial. There's lots of in-depth, original and practical material here, with a focus on child education and health.

A typical issue of *Junior* has 132 colourfully illustrated perfect-bound pages of which about a third are advertisements, including a substantial 'Junior marketplace' section with classified ads for appropriate products ranging from hand-made shoes to innovative clothing to organic nappies.

Each issue of *Junior* carries a well-thought-out mix of practical advice, investigative features, and humour. There are regular columns on family matters, physical and psychological health and development, learning at home, medical matters, shopping, travel, motoring, the working lives of parents ... pretty well everything you need to know about bringing up children while staying sane and living a full life too. There's also a substantial section devoted to children's fashion, the brands featured reflecting the social and financial status of the magazine's core readership: Baby Gap, Young Versace, Dior, D&G Junior, Ralph Lauren ... And there's a 'frank and funny' problem page by 'alternative expert' Kate Konopicky ('giving the answers no health visitor ever would').

In one issue we reviewed, there were half a dozen features on such varied topics as, among others, 'The hospital visitor on four legs - pet therapy for sick children', 'Left-handers: Does it matter what hand your child writes with?' and 'From sex toys to surgery ... the mothers who say their sex life is better than ever'.

This issue had three short humorous features, two of them written by fathers: 'The first meal out with children', a dad's eye view of 'Frills, frou-frou and fancy frocks', and 'We will rock you': how children change the way you interact with music.

The same issue also had an 18-page creative education special.

Editor Catherine O'Dolan will consider ideas *in writing* for main features of 2,000 to 3,000 words, and will look at short, humorous articles of 800 words. (It would be best to submit the whole ms for these short pieces, I suggest, as it's difficult to assess humour from just an idea.)

Tip: It's vital to know the magazine well before you offer anything. The style is upbeat and positive, the writing high quality yet both informal and accessible - and the competition is fierce.

KIDS ALIVE!

Editor: Major Ken Nesbitt

The Salvation Army, 101 Newington Causeway, London SE1 6BN.

Tel: 020 7367 4911. Fax: 020 7367 4710.

E-mail: kidsalive@salvationarmy.org.uk

Website: www.salvationarmy.org.uk/kidsalive

Weekly, 20p. Founded 1881. Circulation a. Publishes non-fiction and short fiction. Query advisable. Pay band A, on acceptance and after submission of an invoice.

Previously known as *The Young Soldier*, *Kids Alive!* is the Salvation Army's weekly magazine for children. It is bright, lively and cheerful - and not exclusively religious in content. It is aimed not just at Army kids, but at *all* children in the age range about 7 to 12. *Kids Alive!* is distributed/sold at Army centres and on the streets, and is available by subscription.

Kids Alive! contains either eight or twelve colourful pages in alternate weeks. There are no advertisements. The magazine's style is very much that of a comic - much is in picture-script format.

The front page is always topical, the back cover is always an amusing comic strip story; there is always a centre-page spread of cartoons, jokes and puzzles; there is always a page of *Kids Alive!* Club activities and news, another of Army children's activities, and another devoted to the 'Postal Sunday School'. In every issue there is a Bible story re-told, in modern idiom, in picture-script. And there is usually at least one article about something of interest, or things to make or do, a 'fact-file' (on a single subject, ranging from 'Mums' to the Romans) and a thought-provoking competition, for worthwhile prizes.

In the larger issues, there are usually more pages of interesting information. Again, these are usually in comic-style, eight-to-ten frame, picture-script form. The factual articles are always plentifully illustrated and they are often in the form of mini-series.

The Editor of *Kids Alive!* welcomes contributions to the central puzzle pages, ideas (only, initially) for possible picture-scripts - non-fiction or fiction - and if within your capabilities, maybe even contributions for the Postal Sunday School. It is even more important than usual, though, to study several copies of the magazine before offering work - *it's different*. Send the Editor a large s.a.e. and he'll probably send you a couple of sample back issues for free.

Remember. if writing picture-script material, you don't have to draw the pictures, merely describe their content and script the dialogue within. There are more details about picture-scripting on page 138.

It's a small and very busy editorial office at *Kids Alive!* but you'll usually get a response to submissions or queries within two or three weeks. They're nice people to work with.

Tip: Subscription details are on the website, which is lively and colourful - well worth a look.

THE LADY

Editor: Arline Usden

Features Editor: Janina Pogorzelski

39-40 Bedford Street, London WC2E 9ER.

Tel: 020 7379 4717. Editorial fax: 020 7836 4620.

E-mail: editors@lady.co.uk   Website: www.lady.co.uk

Weekly, 80p. Founded 1885. Circulation a. Publishes non-fiction and fiction (short stories). Pay band C, at the end of the month of publication.

The longest-established weekly women's magazine, *The Lady* has kept up with the times, but always tastefully. Its readership has not changed much; they are readily identifiable as gentle, affluent and 40-plus.

Advertisements fill nearly two-thirds of the pages, about 10 of these showing display ads for holiday houses and hotels, nursing homes, charities, clothes, flowers ... and stair lifts. The rest of the advert pages carry *The Lady's* renowned classified ads for holiday houses and hotels (in the UK and abroad), for domestic staff ... and it is *the* place for nannies.

A typical issue of *The Lady* has an eclectic mix of features, some black-and-white illustrated, some colour.

Throughout the year, there are special issues focusing on themes like cruising, gardening, pets, health and beauty, money, travel and royal anniversaries.

The editorial pages have several regular features: news of current concerts, operas, festivals, exhibitions etc., advice on gardening and shopping, plus recipes and fashion, answers to readers' queries, book reviews, part-pages on bridge, crosswords and the much-loved 'Ladygram'. Celebrity interviews and a back-page feature, 'Favourite Things', are also regulars. There are usually several one-off features and a short story each week.

Many of the features are staff-written, but articles (thoroughly checked) by freelance contributors are welcome. There is a reader-contributed 'Your Viewpoint' slot, about 450 words long. In one issue we read, the writer contrasted driving in the UK with driving in Europe, contending that the time has come for the UK to convert to driving on the right.

The Lady welcomes one- and two-page articles, 900 and 1,200 words respectively, and ideally with transparencies or photographs, images and copy saved on disk.

Features in one issue we read included: 'Winchester, City of Kings'; 'Mermaids, Myth and Magic' - a trip around the rugged coast of Cornwall; 'The Button-Makers of Dorset'; 'From Dairy Cows to Dinosaurs' - how the discovery of ancient bones in the Isle of Wight cliffs changed the lives of a farming couple; and 'Figures of Fun' - traditional characters from Italian Renaissance comedy. Advance queries/outlines are welcomed by post, only, especially for potential anniversary-based articles, in case someone else has got in first.

MAKING MONEY

The world of opportunities

Editor: Jeff James

Partridge Publications (2000) Ltd, Avenue Lodge, 60 East Street, Brighton BN1 1HN.

Tel: 01273 719900. E-mail: mmedit@partridgeltd.co.uk

Website: www.makingmoney.co.uk

Monthly, £2.45. Founded 1996. Circulation a. Non-fiction only. Query essential. *Don't send short stories or poetry.* Pay band C, on the first of the month following publication.

Making Money is a colourful, lively magazine covering the whole spectrum of business opportunities and start-ups, from high street franchises to network marketing companies, what is available and what it takes to be successful - a wide range of topics to interest everyone who's keen to make money - and who isn't!

Making Money also covers crucial basics like finance, taxation and the law, and keeps its readers up to date on developments in communications, the internet, and technology for small businesses. There are also valuable business-focused readers' giveaways.

A typical issue will have 100 profusely illustrated perfect-bound pages of which about a third will be advertisements for products, services and opportunities relevant to small business ventures. There's a large section on franchising, with lists of websites ('Franfinder') and short articles on specific areas of the franchising world. These are not bylined, so we assume they are sourced in-house.

There are also lists of start-up opportunities, a Redundancy Clinic, and several regular columns, mainly written by regular contributors - of whom at least some are freelance writers.

Of particular interest to the freelance are the half-dozen or so feature articles and interviews in each issue. In one issue we reviewed, we read about 'Tricks of the Trade': secrets of super selling; 'Are medical insurers stitching us up?': 'Talk is cheap': network marketing: 'The confidence ladder': climb your way to success (written by an industry coach); and an interview with top business guru Ron G. Holland.

All the features in *Making Money* are thoroughly researched, factually accurate, and designed to enable and encourage the entrepreneurial spirit. Most include case studies and give leads to further information.

The style is friendly and accessible, the writing concise and polished - no waffle. Study at least two or three issues to get the 'feel'.

The Editor is interested in franchise and network marketing success stories, business opportunities, investment advice, business support and the like - features focused on the magazine's core interest, making money. Make your first approach with ideas, synopses and examples of published work. Don't send full mss.. Length varies according to the scope and depth of each piece, and will be discussed if your idea is taken up.

Making Money is profusely illustrated with high quality pictures - if you can offer photos to support your work, you'll have a better chance.

MORE!

Smart girls get more!

Editor: Marianne Jones

Features Editor: Ceri Roberts

Emap Elan Network, Endeavour House, 189 Shaftesbury Avenue, London WC2H 8JG.

Tel: 020 7208 3165. Fax: 020 7208 3595. E-mail: more.letters@emap.com

Every two weeks, £1.55. Founded 1988. Circulation d. Publishes non-fiction and short fiction. Pay band D, at the end of the month of publication.

Aimed at young women in their late teens to early twenties, *more!* is bright and cheerful, much illustrated and packed with all the things that interest young women in that age bracket. As well as articles about desirable men, relationships and sex, topics such as travel, emotional issues and careers are also covered.

A typical issue of *more!* has about 130 saddle-stitched pages of which about 30 are advertisements, for cosmetics, pharmaceutical products, clothes, magazines, cars, video games, mobile phones and charities. There are also pages devoted to fashion and beauty.

On the editorial side, there are pages of 'Hot gossip', 'Men Unzipped' (including a male centrefold and mainly dealing with men's sexual interests, 'pulling' abilities and the like), sex features, celebrity news features, and photo-sessions-cum-interviews with pop groups and hunky stars. There are two 'agony' columns, one by an 'agony uncle', one by an 'aunt'.

There's a Letters page ('Hot mail' - looking for 'opinionated' letters), half a dozen letters with a prize for the Star letter.

The closing page is titled 'I wish I'd never', and uses about eight letters on the lines of: 'I wish I'd never done it in a public loo'. Each letter printed on this page wins a Polaroid Joycam camera.

In one issue we reviewed, there was a round-up of articles showing how three couples proved that 'Cupid can strike in the most bizarre places'; a feature by a freelance writer on the huge increase in suicide among young men; a one-page piece stating that mates are not necessarily for life; a page suggesting 24 things not to do when you're drunk. Another issue featured three girls whose mothers were meddling too much in their lives, and the same issue had an article asking 'Is Your Beauty Routine Killing You?' - an investigation into toxic ingredients in beauty products. This issue also featured '10 steps to better bonking'.

There are also features and news snippets on celebrities in the appropriate age group.

Much of *more!* is written in a light, sometimes sexually suggestive style, but they do use some more serious material like the 'suicide' piece. The magazine deals confidently and frankly with a wide spectrum of topics that are truly relevant and interesting to the lives of today's young women.

About 40% of the features are commissioned - from a group of well proven freelances - but they are always willing to consider *relevant* ideas on spec.

And there is a regular one-page 'five-minute fiction' slot. By today's standards - Black Lace, etc. - this could be classed as mildly erotic. The preferred length is about 800 words - a real short-short.

MOTHER & BABY

Your No. 1 baby mag

Editor: Dani Zur

Deputy/Features Editor: Una Rice

emap esprit, Greater London House, Hampstead Road, London NW1 7EJ.

Tel: 020 7874 0200.

E-mail: mother&baby@emap.com

Monthly, £1.99. Founded 1956. Circulation b. Publishes non-fiction only. *Don't send short stories or poetry.* Pay band D, at the end of the month of publication.

Mother & Baby magazine has been around for almost fifty years, and all the while has kept itself well and truly up-to-date. It is all about pregnancy, motherhood and babies - and toddlers up to about three years old. Its target readership is obviously young mothers and mothers-to-be: it offers reassurance, advice and information.

A typical issue of *Mother & Baby* will have about 170 bright, colourful saddle-stitched A4 pages of which about half will be advertisements and product promotions. The ads are mainly for child-care pharmaceuticals, baby and toddler food, clothes for both mother and baby, and many *sensible* toys (for toddlers and dads).

Mother & Baby is packed with information, advice and helpful tips on every aspect of parenthood, plus prize competitions and special reader offers.

Editorially, the magazine has several core sections, dealing with pregnancy and birth, bringing up babies and toddlers, development, health, and consumer testing. Within these departments there are many one-off features, often staff-written or by specialist experts but with the possibility of some being by experienced freelance writers.

Every issue of *Mother & Baby* includes several readers' stories about their experiences of pregnancy, birth, and the early years of parenthood, and how they coped with problems, both medical and emotional. These features focus on helping other parents and parents-to-be who might find themselves in similar situations. One issue we reviewed covered diabetes in pregnancy, antenatal depression, and tips on child-proofing your home. There was also a 9-page water-birth special giving both mums' and dads' views on the experience. Another feature looked at the importance of maintaining friendships despite the demands of parenthood.

Articles are usually from 600 to 1,000 words, but can be longer; all have factual sidebars and sources of further advice/information. Writers are not expected to supply the illustrations.

If you have a *relevant* idea for a feature for *Mother & Baby*, send the Features Editor a *brief* outline and some evidence of your parental and writing credentials. If you get the go-ahead, the Features Editor will specify the style and angle the feature should take to fit in with future editorial requirements.

Overall, if you're a young mother or mother-to-be, and a writer, then *Mother & Baby* is well worth a look.

MY WEEKLY

For The Good Things In Life

Editor: Harrison Watson

Features Editor: Sally Hampton

D. C. Thomson & Co Ltd, 80 Kingsway East, Dundee DD4 8SL.

Tel: 01382 223131. Fax: 01382 452491.

Weekly, 58p. Founded 1910. Circulation d. Publishes short stories, serials and story series, celebrity profiles and interviews, and True Life stories. Pay band C, on acceptance.

My Weekly has been around since 1910 - and is still going strong. Its readership is 'young' women of all ages. The target reader age is the mid- to late fifties but *My Weekly* is undoubtedly read by women from their mid-twenties to beyond their sixties.

A typical issue will have about 56 saddle-stitched pages of which 15 or so will be advertisements. The adverts reflect the readership: recliner chairs, loose covers, mail-order clothes and plants and equipment for the garden.

The magazine has several regular features including: health, cooking, knitting or other craft patterns, fashion, plus astrology and 'agony' columns, a prize crossword, and TV news, reviews and interviews. Like many other magazines today, *My Weekly* has a True Life story spot: 'Your Own Page', which offers £50 for a story about 'a special time you'd like to share' - 800-900 words long - plus £5 for every photograph printed.

Most issues have one or two interview-based stories; one issue we reviewed had a profile of actor Ted Danson and an interview with 'At Home With the Braithwaites' star Amanda Redman, plus style tips from singer Jane McDonald.

There is a lively Letters page (including some tips): Write to 'We Love Your Letters', *My Weekly*, 185 Fleet Street, London EC4 2HS - and they ask you to tell them your 3 favourite items in the magazine when you write. They use 6 or 7 letters of up to 150 words each, paying £5 for each one used and £25 for the best of the week.

But it is for its fiction that *My Weekly* is best known. There is always at least one serial running, and the Fiction Editor is also in the market for short-short stories (1,000-1,500 words, possibly off-beat, occasionally twist-in-the-tail) and longer complete stories of up to 4,000 words (2,500 words is the ideal). Story characters can be any age as long as they're *real* and the stories are entertaining. A touch of humour is always welcome. *My Weekly* also considers historical stories. (Note that My *Weekly* readers do *not* enjoy reading about violence or gratuitous sex.)

Each issue of *My Weekly* now also includes a 'Tell It To The Children' short story suitable for reading to the youngsters, 400-500 words long. One story I read was about a mysterious stranger who arrived at a bunnies' birthday party.

Decisions on article queries and short stories come within 6 to 8 weeks. If you're 'nearly there' the people at DCT are well known for being helpful.

Tip: There are comprehensive and detailed guidelines available for *My Weekly* fiction - send an s.a.e.

THE NEW WRITER

Publisher: Merric Davidson

Editor: Suzanne Ruthven. Poetry Editor: Abi Hughes-Edwards

PO Box 60, Cranbrook, Kent TNI7 2ZR. Tel: 01580 212626.

E-mail: admin@thenewwriter.com   Website: www.thenewwriter.com

Every two months, £3.95 (subscription only, £22.50 a year UK, Europe £28.50, RoW £33.00). Founded 1996 by the merging of *Quartos* and *Acclaim*. Circulation a. Publishes non-fiction (all writing-related), poetry and short fiction *(but see below)*. Pay band A, at the end of the month of publication.

The New Writer is targeted at enthusiastic new writers who are willing to work at their craft. It offers its subscribers opportunities to submit their work - fiction, non-fiction and poetry - for criticism and/or possible publication. It is *a friendly* magazine with a 'club-like' atmosphere to it.

A typical issue of *The New Writer* will have 56 A4 saddle-stitched pages; the advertising content is limited and mainly for its own associated services - plus one page of classified ads for other writers' magazines and services.

The editorial content is evenly balanced: a typical issue might contain five or six feature articles, including instructional pieces and interviews, four or five quite lengthy short stories and a six-page section (titled *Diverse)* of poetry and poetry matters. As well as these largely one-offs, there are a number of regular spots: one or two chatty 'opinion' columns, several pages of market and competition news, a regional round-up of what's on, and various other news and information columns.

The editor welcomes 'essays, articles and interviews covering any writing-related or literary theme in its widest sense, up to 2,000 words; longer pieces or series should be proposed by letter in the first instance.' She does not want articles on elementary writing topics like, for example, how to deal with writer's block. Most published articles are more 'creative/literary' than hard 'how-to'.

Unsolicited fiction from non-subscribers is not wanted at all. Some of the stories used in the magazine come from invited guest writers, some are selected runners-up from the major writing competitions, and some come from subscribers' work submitted for criticism. Every story submitted (with s.a.e.) gets back a 'tick-sheet' of criticism and advice - or an offer to publish. Published stories are often quite long, up to 4,000 words, and earn a £10 voucher.

Poetry can be of any reasonable length, must be unpublished, interesting and original and should preferably offer challenging imagery. Each published poem earns £3. Articles about poetry are also welcome.

Initial enquiries can be sent by e-mail, *but no submissions are accepted on disk.* Submissions must be clear, sharp, double-spaced (except for poetry) hard copy only, paper-clipped, and sent by post - for scanning in. They also ask for a 30-word biography with each submission.

Decisions on submissions come within about a month - publication may be much later.

Tip: The New Writer now offers its subscribers a regular free e-mail newsletter, *TNW News Online* - 'meaty beaty big and bouncy'.

19

Barefaced cheek!

Editor: Helen Bazvaye (extension 6410)

Features Editor: Alex Reece (extension 6138)

IPC Southbank Publishing Co Ltd, 29th Floor, King's Reach Tower, Stamford Street, London SE1 9LS.

Tel: 0207 261 5000. Fax: 0207 261 7634. E-mail: 19letters@ipcmedia.com

Monthly, £2.30. Founded 1968. Circulation c. Non-fiction only. Query preferred. *Don't send short stories or poetry.* Pay band C, at the end of the month of publication.

19 is an IPC magazine directed at young women in the 17-24 age group, covering fashion, beauty, relationships, and all the other issues that affect young women today. *19* is a sexy, spirited magazine which handles controversial topics with confidence.

A typical issue of *19* will have around 132 bright, colourful and glossy perfect-bound pages - of which about 35 will be advertisements, for fragrances, fashion, cosmetics and other pharmaceutical products, and cars.

On the editorial side there are several regular sections. Multi-page departments include beauty, fashion (everything from trainers to evening wear) and health (including straight-talking, but not suggestive or smutty, advice on sexual concerns). There are other, smaller regular sections/pages including an opinion spot - by a man - and, of course, horoscopes. There is an agony column and a small Letters page, which includes a 'Joke of the month' and boyfriend photos - 'a photo that just has to be seen'; most letters are back-issue-related, from about 50 to 100 words; the Star letter in one issue we reviewed won a mobile phone. There are quizzes, too, of the 'Are you suffering from cling-on-itis?' type.

There are also several one-off articles in each issue of *19*, including real-life stories. These are articles on general topics of interest to young women in the target age group, ranging from the entertaining and amusing to serious social matters. Many of these are written/compiled by the senior Features Editor herself or by staff feature-writers, but a few one-off features have the bylines of non-staff writers - and are almost certainly commissioned. A few of these one-off features, though, could readily be produced by a freelance - given appropriate ideas and experience. And that stable of regular freelances must have started somehow, somewhere. One potentially freelance-contributed feature in the issue we read was titled 'Stealing Booty' - the rise in street theft of designer goods.

Length required varies according to the weight of the subject, up to about 2,500 words.

The magazine prefers not to look at unsolicited manuscripts but is willing to consider ideas. If you have what you believe is a truly *19*-relevant feature idea, submit it in writing on a single sheet, together with photocopies of just one or two similar published features, if possible. You *might* get a tentative go-ahead. And if you live up to your 'promise', who knows, you *could* find yourself joining that 'stable' of writers who are regularly commissioned by *19*.

Tip: The Editor looks for 'bold, original, vigorous' writing and ideas.

NURSERY WORLD

Editor: Liz Roberts

Deputy Editor: Ruth Thomson

Admiral House, 66-68 East Smithfield, London E1W 1BX.

Tel: 020 7782 3120. Fax: 020 7782 3131.

Website: www.nursery-world.com

Weekly, £1.20. Publishes non-fiction only. *Don't send short stories or poetry.* Pay band C, at the end of the month of publication.

Nursery World is a weekly magazine specifically for professional child-carers (nannies, nursery nurses etc.), teachers and support staff associated with children up to eight years old. It is also of interest to parents - but, being a magazine for professionals, it is not in the same mould as the more lay-interest parenting magazines.

A typical issue of *Nursery World* will have 36 saddle-stitched, full colour illustrated pages of which about a dozen will be advertisements. Half the advertisements will be classified ads - for nannies' job vacancies and wanted; display adverts include resources and equipment, organisations (including trade unions) and private sector and local authority job ads.

On the editorial side there are several regular pages of news and forthcoming events. There is a lively but strictly professional Letters page, the majority of the letters back-issue related. and there are one-off features and series covering child care, education, health - virtually any aspect of bringing up children.

There will be one-off specialist features in most issues of the magazine. Some of these will be either staff-produced or too specialised to be within reach of the *general* freelance. There are, though, usually one or two features in each issue that could be produced by a freelance with general experience in the broad child-care profession - which could be said to embrace many mothers. But the *slant* of any such feature must be very much from a professional viewpoint rather than that of a parent.

In the most recent issue we reviewed, there was a feature looking at the need for both early years practitioners and parents to be aware of the essentials of both emotional and physical care; this piece included a 'Cut out and photocopy' page titled 'A parent's guide to the essentials'. The same issue had a 4-page pull-out of nursery activities, with a collection of projects - ideas for such projects are welcome.

All features are illustrated, and most have quite lengthy, fact-packed, informative sidebars, too.

The Editor of *Nursery World* is happy to consider brief outlines for *relevant* - and appropriately slanted - features. Decisions come fairly quickly, usually within a couple of weeks.

THE PEOPLE'S FRIEND

The Famous Story Magazine

Editor: Margaret McCoy

Features Editor: Hilary Lyall

D. C. Thomson & Co Ltd, 80 Kingsway East, Dundee DD4 8SL.

Tel: 01382 462276. Fax: 01382 452491.

Weekly, 58p. Founded 1869. Circulation d. Publishes mainly fiction (short stories and serials), articles and poetry. *Query essential for articles.* Pay band A, on acceptance.

Working to a highly successful formula – plenty of good, entertaining stories – *The People's Friend* is still extremely popular, having kept up with the times while holding true to its core readership, no mean feat in these days of shifting loyalties. Its readership includes women of all ages, from 30 to 80-plus, but it is perhaps more specifically targeted on the 50-plus.

A typical issue of *The People's Friend* has about 70-plus colourful but never 'brash' pages, of which about a third are advertisements. The adverts, reflecting the readership, are mainly for mail-order clothes, recliner chairs, stair lifts, decorative plates, plants for the garden, and charities.

Editorially, there are always such favourites as knitting patterns, recipes, health, gardening, and answers to readers' factual queries (*not* an 'agony' column). There is a feature about the beauty-spot pictured on the cover, and a (freelance-contributed) illustrated travel piece about an interesting place somewhere in the UK. Check with the Features Editor before submitting anything. 'Your letters and pictures' uses 8 or 9 letters each week, up to 200 words, each winning a tea-caddy prize, with a bigger prize for the week's best. 'Snap Happy' welcomes photos: half a dozen each week on one topic (one issue we reviewed had 7 snaps under the title Cats' Chorus!) paying £5 for each snap published. Photos can only be returned if you enclose an s.a.e.

Most issues include at least one potentially freelance-contributed feature article – about 1,000 words with a photo or two. Topics range from first-person holiday experiences to places remembered from childhood. One contribution we read told of a NAAFI volunteer's experiences on the island of Cyprus.

There are poems in most issues of *The People's Friend*, all short, 'traditional' (i.e., rhyming and scanning) with a clear meaning or message.

But it is for its stories that *The People's Friend* is best known. In addition to one or two serial episodes, each issue usually has about half a dozen short stories. One, 500-700 words long, is for the children – nursery/primary age. The others range from 1,000 to 4,000 words; the most popular length is about 2,000 to 3,000 words. Stories can include characters of any age and should be light-hearted and heart-warmingly emotional; they should leave the readers with a good feeling. Twist-in-the-tail stories are seldom wanted. Avoid the supernatural and explicit sex or violence. The Editor is also interested in fiction series; details are in the guidelines – see below.

Be prepared to wait a few weeks for a decision. Every submission is carefully read, and DCT editors are renowned for their helpful attitude to 'almost there' writers.

Tip: The Editor advises that you study the magazine well before submitting, and try your hand at short stories before attempting other formats. Send only one story at a time – if they want to see more, they'll ask. Detailed and specific guidelines are available – send an s.a.e.

PRACTICAL FAMILY HISTORY

Family history – pure and simple

Managing Editor: Sue Fearn

Editor: Peter Watson

61 Great Whyte, Ramsey, Huntingdon PE26 1HJ.

Tel: 01487 814050 (8.30 am to 4.30 pm Monday to Friday).

Fax: 01487 711361. E-mail: Lesboon@family-tree.co.uk

Website: www.family-tree.co.uk

Monthly, £2.20. Founded 1997. Circulation a. Non-fiction only. *Don't send short stories or poetry.* Pay band A, at the end of the month of publication.

Practical Family History is a special interest magazine and its inclusion in the *Handbook* might therefore be thought inappropriate – but we all have (or have had) families and most of us are at least vaguely interested in our own history. So ... it's included.

Practical Family History is a sister magazine to the well-established – and very specialist – *Family Tree Magazine*. It is, however, aimed at the less experienced, amateur family historian. A typical issue will have 60 saddle-stitched pages attractively illustrated in both colour and black-and-white; there are only a few pages of advertisements – mostly relating to family tree research.

The magazine has resident experts who contribute various regular columns about family history sources and specific research methods – including what in another context would be called an 'agony' column (questions and answers). As well as the resident experts, there are openings for several freelance contributions in each issue.

Typical feature subjects in one issue we reviewed included 'British heralds and their duties'; 'Memorials in unusual places'; 'The Poor Law system in Scotland after 1845'; 'The wealth of information in obits' ('Don't overlook the obituary pages'); 'A transportation tale: the story of the first Newgate convicts to be transported'; and 'Trades from the past: Framework knitters in the East Midlands'.

Length varies from half a page (400-500 words) to almost 2 pages (about 2,000 words). Most pieces are illustrated, with old black-and-white or sepia photographs. *Practical Family History* pays on wordage rather than space, though - nothing for photographs.

Don't submit original early photographs. Make a photographic copy – not a photocopy – and send that. And beware copyright on old photographs. The magazine reckons 70 years is long enough to be free of copyright; we would recommend 100 years: the copyright owner might have been young when the picture was taken – the rule is 70 years after death.

Unless you are already an expert in family genealogy, don't try offering technical articles – but there is scope for occasional articles along the lines of unusual sources of information, or how you overcame a problem while uncovering your own family history.

Decisions on submitted material can take 3 or 4 months at busy times. And be prepared for a long delay after acceptance for publication.

Tip: If you *are* an expert in any aspect of genealogy, you might also be able to write for 'big sister', *Family Tree Magazine* – which has been going for nearly twenty years and is read by over 100,000 people world-wide.

PRACTICAL HOUSEHOLDER

The UK's leading DIY magazine

Editor: John McGowan

Highbury wViP, 53-79 Highgate Road, London NW5 1TW.

Tel: 01322 660070 ext. 2373. Fax: 020 7331 1269.

E-mail: john.mcgowan@nexusmedia.com

Website: www.nexusonline.com

Monthly, £2.50. Founded 1955. Circulation a. Non-fiction only. *Query essential.* Pay band A, at the end of the month of publication.

The target readership of *Practical Householder* is abundantly clear – the usually male, practical (that lets Gordon out, he says) householder, aged anywhere between 20 and 80, willing and able to do jobs around the house and garden himself (or herself).

A typical issue of *Practical Householder* now has 100 colourful saddle-stitched A4 pages of which about a dozen will be advertisements. The adverts offer DIY tools and equipment, replacement doors, etc., ready-to-install improvements and various items of household equipment. There are numerous staff-tested equipment assessments throughout the magazine.

The editorial pages of *Practical Householder* are packed with photographic and/or drawn step-by-step illustrations of various DIY activities – from putting up shelving to creating a stream in your garden.

Many of the one-off features are freelance-contributed, but the writers are usually part of a regular and established 'stable' of proven experts. If, however, you are an expert at some aspect of household or garden improvement work, you might get lucky. Most editors welcome additional competent experts into their existing 'stables'.

There do appear to be occasional opportunities for writers to provide how-to material. One issue we reviewed included, under the section heading 'Crafts for the home', a detailed feature on 'The art of deception' – using trompe l'oeil stencilling in the home; the piece gave information on every aspect of the project, from materials required to creating the art forms; the same issue also had a feature on choosing and using floor-coverings.

All the how-to features have detailed step-by-step instruction, some tasks are graded 'basic', 'medium' or 'advanced' skill, and all are profusely illustrated (not necessarily by the writer); most include sidebars listing essential tools, materials needed, suppliers etc. Features go up to about 2,000 words, inclusive of sidebars.

Each issue of *Practical Householder* also includes one or two shorter how-to features, each less than a page, often just step-by-step illustrations plus explanatory captions. These deal mainly with smaller jobs around the house and garden. Offering a picture-script and captions for one of these spots might be a good way of introducing yourself to the Editor – but even then, start off with a *brief* outline/query. Decisions usually come within two to three weeks.

There is also a letters-cum-tips page – write to 'Passing It On' – using half-a-dozen money-saving tips or DIY anecdotes each month. Letters are paraphrased by the Editor, and the two best get valuable DIY-related prizes.

PRACTICAL PARENTING

Incorporating Practical Parenting's Complete Guide to Pregnancy

Editor-in-Chief: Jayne Marsden

Deputy Editor: Anne Hunt (020 7261 7234)

PA: Tracey Wells (020 7261 5058)

IPC Media Ltd, King's Reach Tower, Stamford Street, London SE1 9LS.

Monthly, £2.30. Founded 1987. Circulation c. Non-fiction only. Query advisable. *Don't send short stories or poetry.* Pay band D, at the end of the month of publication.

Practical Parenting is a well established IPC monthly magazine for parents with children ranging from 0 to 5 years, and for mums-to-be, particularly first-timers – a clear and specific target readership.

A typical issue of *Practical Parenting* has about 132 bright and colourful perfect-bound pages of which about 40 per cent are adverts for medicines and toiletries, food for babies and toddlers, nappies, nursery equipment and the like – and good sensible toys for babies and toddlers.

Editorially, there are several regular sections/departments written by the magazine's team of experts, dealing with pregnancy and birth, child development, baby- and child-care, health, pre-school education – and cooking. There are several pages of giveaways and several of equipment tests – in one issue we reviewed, this section included reusable nappies, safety gates, and breastfeeding 'must-haves'.

There is a Letters page, inviting readers to share their 'views, tips and stories' – no payment or prizes offered.

Practical Parenting publishes several parents' stories in each issue, including regular 'Pregnancy Diaries' in which three mums-to-be record their experiences, thoughts and feelings at different stages of pregnancy.

There are also many one-off features in each month's *Practical Parenting*. Most are by experts, like the one debating the MMR vaccine controversy, but some could be by 'ordinary' freelance writers experienced in caring for very young children. The issue we reviewed included a feature titled 'My little miracles', a mother's account of carrying and delivering conjoined twins. In the same issue, other possibly freelance-written features were '20 ways to boost your toddler's confidence' and a 'round-up' feature titled 'Little or large – Four mums tell us what their family size means to them'; the latter piece was accompanied by snapshots of the featured families.

Lengths vary widely, up to about 3,000 words maximum. If you have an idea for a really relevant feature for *Practical Parenting*, submit a *brief* outline and hope for a go-ahead.

Most photographs are taken by commissioned photographers.

The issue we reviewed also had a back-page 'Family travel' piece featuring two families' experiences of holidays in the UK: one family took a farmhouse break in Kent, the other stayed at a bungalow on the Norfolk coast. Each of these short features was about 250 words plus a fact file and two snapshots. If you've had a fun family holiday, it might be worth offering a piece for this spot.

Tip: All material must be written with the magazine's very specific target readership in mind.

PRIMA

Live well for less

Editor: Maire Fahey

PA: Sandra Tear

The National Magazine Co Ltd, 197 Marsh Wall, London E14 9SG.

Tel: 020 7519 5500. E-mail: prima@natmags.co.uk

Website: www.primamagazine.co.uk

Monthly, £2.00. Founded 1986. Circulation d. Non-fiction only. *Don't send short stories or poetry.* Pay band D, at the end of the month of publication.

Prima is a very practical magazine – full of lots of things to make and do. It is aimed at women of all ages, but the 'core' readership is probably those in the 25 to 50 age bracket.

A typical issue of *Prima* will have about 148 bright and colourful saddle-stitched pages, of which a good third will be advertisements. The adverts – for foodstuffs, clothes, cosmetics and pharmaceutical products, among other things – bear out the target reader-age suggested above. Its practicality, too, is borne out not only by the editorial sections/departments, but also by the paper sewing pattern that is always bound into the magazine. (In one issue we reviewed, the pattern included outfits for a bridal gown, and dresses for bridesmaids and a flower girl, a beaded bag, plus a cravat for the groom.) The same issue also showed how to cover books, notebooks and boxes with fabric.

Editorially, *Prima* includes major sections on fashion, beauty-care, home-making, cooking (with cut-out-and-keep recipes), gardening, finance, an 'agony' column, astrology pages, a prize crossword puzzle, and special reader offers. There's a regular travel spot, usually several small 'info-bites', and a 'Prima Kids' page with an advice 'Q & A' and news of appropriate new products. A 'Lucky Number' competition offers a top prize of £20,000, with substantial cash prizes for 32 others.

There's a Letters page with 8 or 9 back-issue-related letters each month – earning £25 for the Star letter and a subscription to *Prima* for each of the others.

Prima now includes a 'Mind, body and soul' section, covering physical and emotional health and well-being. In the issue we reviewed, this section included 'I saved my husband's life: How three women helped their partners recover from serious illnesses', and 'Seize the moment: Stop procrastinating and start acting, for a happier life'.

Study several *recent* issues before you offer anything, then send an outline of your idea to the Editor. Your best chance would probably lie with short, illustrated features with a 'how to do it' approach. If you put up a really *Prima*-relevant idea, they may get back to you. If the idea's not right, they probably won't.

Most *Prima* features are commissioned from established writers and specialists, though, so you would need to know your subject thoroughly.

The Magazine Writer's Handbook

PROSPECT

Politics, essays, argument

Editor: David Goodhart

Assistant Editor: Lucy Roeber

4 Bedford Square, London WC1B 3RD.

Tel: 020 7255 1281. Fax: 020 7255 1279.

E-mail: editorial@prospect-magazine.co.uk

Website: www.prospect-magazine.co.uk

Monthly, £3.80. Founded 1995. Circulation a. Publishes non-fiction – query advisable. Also publishes occasional short fiction. *No poetry*. Pay band C, at the end of the month of publication.

A political and cultural monthly, *Prospect* has established itself as a recognised forum for intelligent and vigorous comment on politics and current affairs, national and international. Content is varied and wide-ranging, and includes essays, opinion and analysis, features, reviews and reports, a letters page – and a challenging crossword puzzle.

Each issue has columns by regular contributors like Edward Chancellor, Toby Mundy and Alexander Linklater, and 14 or 15 one-off features. In two issues we reviewed, these features included: 'Enron and the press – Journalists failed to spot the Enron bubble'; 'The Foster Fix – Norman's conquest of British architecture'; 'The Sun also rises – (The Sun newspaper) has become socially respectable but remains politically pivotal ...'; 'Modern parents – Bringing up children is harder than ever ...' There is also a two-hander debate; in the issues we read, the topics discussed were 'Are global poverty and inequality getting worse?' (Robert Wade vs Martin Wolf), and 'Are young British artists nincompoops and frauds?' (Brian Sewell vs Matthew Collings).

The Editor provides a feast for the thinking reader. He will consider quality submissions, but warns in his guidelines for unsolicited submissions: 'Almost without exception, all the articles in *Prospect* are commissioned from our regular writers. We very rarely publish unsolicited submissions and we may take up to three months to respond to them. Before submitting an article, please read the magazine to make sure that your piece is suitable for *Prospect*.'

Prospect uses three main types of articles. Briefly:

Opinions (750 to 1,200 words) expressing 'a well argued and concise point about politics, current events or culture.'

Essays (4,000 to 6,000 words) presenting 'a more developed point, usually from an authoritative or knowledgeable source, or from a viewpoint not conventionally expressed.'

Reviews (600 to 1,500 words) providing 'a critical opinion about a recent book or a recent trend in the arts.'

Prospect also publishes short stories (3,000 to 7,000 words) but only four or five a year and generally by established writers.

Submissions by e-mail are preferred, included in the body of the e-mail, not attached, and sent to: lucy@prospect-magazine.co.uk ... or submissions can be sent by post, to Lucy Roeber at the above address. Full submission guidelines are on the website.

Tip: You would be wise to study several issues of *Prospect* before offering anything.

THE RAILWAY MAGAZINE

A passion for rail: modern & steam in one magazine

Editor: Nick Pigott

Deputy Editor: Chris Milner

King's Reach Tower, Stamford Street, London SE1 9LS.

Tel: 020 7261 5533. Fax: 020 7261 5269. E-mail: railway@ipcmedia.com

Monthly, £3.05. Founded 1897. Circulation a. Publishes non-fiction only. Query advisable for features. *Don't send short stories or poetry.* Pay band C, at the end of the month of publication.

Published by IPC Country & Leisure Media, *The Railway Magazine* targets rail enthusiasts of all ages. The magazine covers modern and heritage railways, steam preservation and railway history – any railway-related subject.

A typical issue of *The Railway Magazine* will have 108 profusely illustrated saddle-stitched pages of which about 20 will be advertisements, for books, videos, rallies and events, auctions, rail-interest holidays and tours, plus several pages of classified adverts for a wide range of services, books and 'railwayana'.

Editorially, there are several regular sections, including a letters page, 'Readers' Platform', that rewards the writer of every published letter with two free Jessops colour transparency films. One issue we reviewed used 15 letters, from about 60 to 200-plus words, many back-issue-related, two with photographs. The issue opened with nine pages of 'Headline News', and later in the magazine there's a 36-page news digest under the umbrella heading 'Track Record'; this section covers news on Steam, Narrow Gauge, Traction & Stock, Metro News, Classic Traction, Rail Tourer, Fight for Freight, Operations News and Traction Update, and includes timetables for steam tours and modern and classic traction tours. The Steam News section includes a portfolio of selected readers' photographs under the heading 'Panorama'.

The features in the issue we read focused on: The Llangollen Railway's plans for the future; the story of the North British Locomotive Company's main line diesel products, marking the anniversary of the last BR loco; 'Monsters of the Midlands', the LMS Garratts, articulated giants which once graced the Midland Main Line; and 'Technicolour Dreamcoats', a guide through the 'livery jungle'. There was also an episode of 'Practice & Performance', a continuing survey of turbine-driven locomotives; and 'Panorama' (mentioned above), sponsored by Fuji Sensia II film, a selection of photographs credited to readers – in this issue, there were five photographs showcased. Each month, 30 rolls of process paid 36-exposure Fuji Sensia II are divided equally among those whose work appears in the 'Panorama' pages. The free film rolls are awarded in addition to *The Railway Magazine*'s reproduction fees. Top quality photographs will be considered for this section.

If you have ideas for features on any British railway subject, whether current or historical, and can offer quality photographic illustrations – colour transparencies preferred, black and white for historical photos – it's best to contact the Editor before completing the article, to check interest. Preferred length for finished features is 1,500 to 2,000 words.

News reports and recent pictures from the current rail network are welcome, as are reports and pictures from recent rail tours (with sketch maps of routes where appropriate), heritage and conservation events, and galas.

READER'S DIGEST

The world's favourite magazine

Editor-in-Chief: Katherine Walker

Deputy Editor: Veronica Pratt

Deputy Editor (Features): Susannah Hickling

11 Westferry Circus, Canary Wharf, London E14 4HE.

Tel: 020 7715 8000. E-mail: theeditor@readersdigest.co.uk

Website: www.readersdigest.co.uk

Monthly, £2.50. Founded 1922. Circulation 25 million in 19 languages worldwide. *Does not accept article-length stories, fiction, cartoons or poetry.* Payment code D, made at the end of the month of publication.

Reader's Digest is not a potential market for 'ordinary' freelance writers. That is not to say that they don't commission work from professional freelances: they do, but they have very specific requirements. It is, though, a marvellous market – and encourages submissions – for true anecdotes, quotes and jokes.

A typical issue of *Readers' Digest* will consist of about 170 A5-sized perfect-bound pages of which about 30 per cent will be advertisements – from exotic holidays to stair lifts, medicines to investment opportunities, cars to packaged food – reflecting the universal nature of the readership. Editorially, there are fifteen to twenty one-off features and a 'Bonus Read' (a long, true-life feature) in each issue.

Of far greater interest to the 'ordinary' freelance writer are the well-paid anecdote/joke/filler/quote items:

- 'Life's Like That': true, unpublished personal experience stories, revealing human nature and humorous or appealing incidents from everyday life – the Editor likes about 300 words, typewritten, in letter form, which can be edited down to about 100 words. They pay £200 each.

- 'All in a Day's Work': true, unpublished stories about humour in the workplace – same length, same pay.

- 'Just Kidding': life through a child's eyes, pay as above.

- 'Laughter, the Best Medicine': jokes, your own or (first report) heard on radio/TV or seen in print. £125 each – about 100 words.

- 'That's Outrageous!': 'If you've heard or read about something outrageous, write and tell us or send the press cutting'. £150 is paid for each 'outrage' used.

Keep checking the magazine – opportunities like these change from time to time, so you need to keep up to date. Send contributions – including your name, address and daytime telephone number on each sheet – for any of the above, marked EXCERPTS. Published material should also include source, date and page number. *Reader's Digest* will neither acknowledge nor return any such submissions and decisions can take several months. Rejections are not notified and payment is made on publication: do not, therefore, offer the same material elsewhere for about six months.

Tip: An excellent booklet, *Writing for Reader's Digest*, is available from the above address: £4.50 by post.

RED

For the best things in life

Editor: Trish Halpin

Deputy Editor: Hero Brown

emap élan Network, Endeavour House, 189 Shaftesbury Avenue, London WC2H 8JG.

Tel: 020 7208 3358. Fax: 020 7208 3218. Website: www.redmagazine.co.uk

Monthly, £2.80. Founded 1998. Circulation c. Publishes non-fiction only. *Don't send short stories or poetry.* Pay band D, at the end of the month of publication.

Red is a big, glossy, stylish magazine for women who want 'the best things in life', as it promises on its cover. *Red*'s target readership is women in their thirties who want an interesting and informative read as well as 'finger-on-the-pulse' news about fashion, beauty, and health. The magazine, though, will undoubtedly attract bright women of all ages and levels of affluence. Its fashion pages, for instance, cater for a wide range of income by showing a thoughtful balance of both designer (expensive) and upper-end-of-the-High-Street (affordable) clothes.

A typical issue of *Red* will have about 220/230 pages, of which around one third will be advertisements. The adverts provide a strong picture of the magazine's target readership: clothes, cars, leather goods, jewellery, perfume, pharmaceutical and beauty products, food and books.

Editorially, *Red* has several regular sections: fashion, health and beauty, food, home and garden, and travel; a horoscope page; and a Letters page, with 5 or 6 usually back-issue-related letters each month, the Star letter receiving a gift – in the issue we reviewed, the gift was a double pack of champagne.

Of most interest to the freelance writer, though: there are 8 or 9 feature articles in every issue of *Red*. In one issue we reviewed, articles covered topics as diverse as, among others, an interview with film star Kristin Scott Thomas; 'It's all Rush, Rush, Rush – Just what's so good about being busy all the time?'; 'Second-Hand Man – Second-Rate Relationship? – When is dealing with a new partner's past more trouble than it's worth?'; 'The Secret Life of the Yo-Yo Dieter'; rethinking spending habits; the rise of drug use at dinner parties; '10 ways to banish a bad mood' (a round-up of tips from ten professional women).

This is not a market for beginners; most features are written by established freelances and 'name' contributors. However, if you have already been published in magazines at a similar level, the Editor will consider ideas for articles likely to interest intelligent women of 30-plus: investigative features, first-person pieces and interviews.

Red's standard is high, and features must be well written and thoroughly investigated, original, and 2,000 to 2,500 words maximum. You would be wise to study several *recent* issues before making any approach. If you have something you feel would interest *Red*'s discriminating readership, submit a detailed proposal by post, together with relevant cuttings or other evidence of published work.

Red is not an easy market to break into, but it's a worthwhile and increasingly prestigious one.

SAGA MAGAZINE

The magazine of the Saga Club

Editor: Emma Soames

Saga Publishing Ltd, The Saga Building, Middelburg Square, Folkestone, Kent CT20 1AZ.

Tel: 01303 771523. Fax: 01303 776699. E-mail: editor@saga.co.uk

Website: www.saga.co.uk/magazine/

Monthly, £2 – available on subscription only, £15.95 a year. (For subscription details phone 01303 771526 or see the Saga website.) Founded 1984. Circulation e. Publishes non-fiction only. Query essential. *Don't send short stories or poetry.* Pay band D, at the end of the month of publication.

Saga Magazine is the magazine of the Saga Club, which is closely associated with Saga Holidays and other companies within the Saga Group. (Saga offers a wide range of other services nowadays, from insurance and health-care to credit cards and investment advice.)

A typical issue of *Saga Magazine* has 196 saddle-stitched pages of which about 25% are advertisements. The adverts range from garden kneelers to mail-order clothes to computers – and many of the extensive range of Saga services. Within the advert element of the magazine there are always details of various Saga holidays on offer. Saga offers its services exclusively to those over 50 – the magazine is aimed at lively, active, and relatively affluent people of both sexes in that age group.

Saga Magazine has many regular sections or columns, some by 'household names' like Keith Waterhouse, Clement Freud, Angela Rippon, Michael Brunson, Marguerite Patten and Katharine Whitehorn, among others. There are pages on gardening, health, motoring, finance, home economics and many other topics of interest to the target readership.

There is a lively Letters section, with more than two dozen letters in each issue – they pay £50 for the month's best, £10 for the rest. Photographs earn extra. 'My Favourite Poem' wins £20 (poems by established poets only).

In addition to the regular features, each issue has a number of one-off articles, mostly profiles-cum-interviews with interesting people within the 'Saga age group'. Length is 1,200 to 1,600 words, with colour illustrations usually provided or arranged by the magazine. A typical issue would have 15 or more such articles. Subjects in issues we've read have included J. K. Rowling of 'Harry Potter' fame, Sophia Loren, changing times in Gibraltar, the tragedy of the Kursk, the filming of The Lord of the Rings, and an interview with pop star Sting.

Although most features are either staff-written or commissioned from regulars, some are undoubtedly provided by freelance writers – maybe one or two per issue. If you have adequate writing experience and know someone of 50-plus with a really interesting story, send a detailed outline to the Editor. *Don't* send the complete manuscript with your first approach. You should get a response within a month – if they're interested in your story, you could be asked to submit the feature on spec.

Tip: Take a warm, personal approach, writing in an upbeat and positive style.

THE SCOTS MAGAZINE

The World's Top-Selling Scottish-Interest Title

Editor: John Methven

D. C. Thomson & Co Ltd, 2 Albert Square, Dundee DD1 9QJ.

Tel: 01382 223131 extension 4119. Fax: 01382 322214.

E-mail: mail@scotsmagazine.com Website: www.scotsmagazine.com

Monthly, £1.35. Founded 1739. Circulation b. Mostly non-fiction – there's an occasional short story. *Queries preferred*. Pay band A: on acceptance for text, on publication for photographs.

The Scots Magazine is a magazine about Scots people, places, history and culture. Its target readership is clear: people who love Scotland, wherever they live in the world. Of both sexes and of all ages but leaning towards the more mature. You don't have to be a Scot to write for it – although judging by many of the contributors' names, I guess it helps – but you have to write about Scotland and things Scottish.

A typical issue of *The Scots Magazine* will have about 112 perfect-bound A5 pages with lots of colour. Of these, about 30 pages will be taken up by advertisements – for hotels and holiday accommodation in Scotland, for Scottish ephemera and such services as ancestor research, for tourist-geared shops, for new homes in Scotland, and for Scottish-based charities.

On the editorial side there are a number of regular sections: Scotland-related book and music reviews, news of what's on in Scotland, comments on the origins of Scottish words, and a thriving but non-paying Letters page – longish letters, mainly back-issue-related.

There are several sections of attractive colour photographs (picture-postcard-like) and many freelance-supplied one-off features.

The preferred length for articles is 1,000 to 2,500 words – and *everything* must be Scotland-related. The magazine's main areas of interest include history, folklore, the outdoors, reminiscence, personalities and wildlife. Nearly all features are illustrated – more in high-quality colour than in black-and-white; for colour, they prefer original transparencies of 35mm and upward.

In one issue we reviewed, there were features on Fred Hunt, 'a world expert in the growing and presentation of alpine plants for showing', written by his friend Ron Thompson and illustrated with Fred Hunt's own photographs; the lighthouse at Start Point, Sanday, written and illustrated by Roderick Thorne; a profile of champion canoeist Alistair Wilson; Ballachulish Slate Quarry; an interview with folk singer Paddie Bell; the changing role of farmers' wives; the history of Mar Lodge Estate; an interview with Annie and Brian Sutherland, who run the organisation 'Games Old and New' which promotes children's play and games in schools, at galas and festivals, and other venues from Orkney to the Borders; a piece on the 300th anniversary of the execution of Scotland's most infamous pirate, Captain William Kidd; an online delve into Scottish history; and a photo-feature on the Solway Firth ... a fascinating variety of topics.

The staff will be pleased to discuss ideas (by letter or e-mail). Just make sure anything you offer is Scotland-related. Editorial decisions come quickly, usually within ten days.

Tip: Helpful and detailed editorial guidelines are available; send an s.a.e.

SHE

Hearts, Minds & Shopping

Editor: Eve Cameron

PA to the Editor: Charlotte Carter

Features Editor: Cayte Williams

National Magazine House, 72 Broadwick Street, London W1F 9EP.

Tel: 020 7439 5000. Website: www.she.co.uk

Monthly, £2.60. Founded 1955. Circulation c. Non-fiction only. *Query essential. Do not send any unsolicited material – it will not be considered nor will it be returned.* Pay band D, at the end of the month of publication.

She is an upmarket magazine for women in the 25-45 age bracket: affluent, stylish, probably working (certainly with a full life), an enthusiastic home-maker, probably 50% have kids – and very interested in their own sensuality. The *She* ethos is stated on the website: 'A spirited mix of honesty, style and humour - *She* empathises with and inspires busy modern women to get the most out of life.'

A typical issue of *She* will have about 192 glossy, perfect-bound pages of which almost half can be advertisements – for cosmetics, fashions, kids' clothes and medication, foodstuffs (including pet foods), pharmaceuticals, household equipment, books and cars.

Editorially, there are regular sections covering fashion and beauty, health and well-being, living and food (including some mouth-watering recipes), relationships and family matters. There are columns covering entertainment, books, travel and astrology, and several reader offers.

There's a Letters page, 'She mail' – half a dozen letters a month, nearly all back-issue-related; all letters printed receive a prize, with an extra-value prize for each month's best.

There are also, of course, several one-off features in each issue of *She*. BUT ... *She*'s editorial policy is crystal clear (although printed in tiny type on the masthead page): **They will not consider unsolicited material at all – nor will they return anything submitted.**

Against that, they don't write all the features in-house; some are from freelances, usually from their 'stable' of known and reliable writers. But that 'stable' must have started somehow, sometime, somewhere. So ... if you have what you think is a particularly *She*-relevant idea, you can try sending them a *brief* written outline/query (plus a photocopy or two of work published in a similar-standard magazine). If they like the outline, they'll get back to you fairly quickly; if not, not at all. Whatever you do, study the magazine thoroughly before putting up an idea.

Typical features in one issue we read included an interview with actress Tamzin Outhwaite; 'How to be a great mum & still have a life'; 'Can you fall in love again (with the man you're already with)?'; 'Love conquers all – Three couples reveal how their relationships were tested to the limits and grew stronger as a result.'

Always worth a good hard try – great magazine, good payers, and they know what their readers want.

TAKE A BREAK

Voted best women's weekly

Editor: John Dale

Fiction Editor: Norah McGrath

H. Bauer Publishing, Academic House, 24-28 Oval Road, London NW1 7DT.

Tel: 020 7241 8000.

Weekly, 66p. Founded 1990. Circulation e. Publishes non-fiction and short fiction. Pay band D, at the end of the month of publication.

Take a Break is a cheerful tabloid-style magazine aimed primarily at women readers but clearly picking up more than a few men too. *Take a Break* has repeatedly been chosen Magazine of the Year. It is rather like its sisters and competitors, *that's life!* and *Chat* – its core readership is women of around 30 but its content is of interest to all ages.

A typical issue of *Take a Break* has around 60 pages of which about 20 per cent are advertisements – for mail-order catalogues, household necessities, pharmaceutical products, and food. On the editorial side, there are several regular sections, dealing with fashion, food, health etc. There is also an astrology feature and several 'problem' pages. There are many reader-participation competitions in every issue – with prizes ranging from £1,000 in cash to a small car. (*Take a Break* Club members have the opportunity to win prizes up to £2,500 in value.)

Editor John Dale has advised us that *Take a Break* magazine is only in the market for stories for their 'Coffee Break' slot - he doesn't want True Life stories, letters and so on from freelance writers, only from *Take a Break* readers. He's happy to consider good short stories, which don't have to be romantic or 'twisters' – 1,000 words maximum. Occasionally, there are two such stories in an issue.

and

TAKE A BREAK'S FICTION FEAST

Editorial staff and address as *Take a Break*.

Monthly, £1.30. Circulation d. Publishes short fiction only. Pay band D, at the end of the month of publication.

Take a Break's Fiction Feast has quickly established itself as a popular leisure-reading magazine – it's good to see a monthly fiction magazine doing well. *Fiction Feast* is packed almost exclusively with short stories in a wide variety of styles and subject matter. The stories should appeal to a wide readership, probably mostly to women, but there were one or two male bylines in the issues we read.

A typical issue of *Fiction Feast* will have 52 saddle-stitched pages of which only two or three will be advertisements, mainly for other *Take a Break* publications.

Editorially, *Fiction Feast* includes one short (under 200 words) book review of the type of novel that would appeal to the same readership as the magazine's short stories. The book reviews are not bylined, but it might be worth your while sending a couple of sample reviews of similar books – you might get taken on as a reviewer. Each issue has a horoscope feature, and there's usually a crossword, a wordsearch puzzle, an arrowword puzzle and a codebreaker puzzle. There are no prizes for the puzzles, other than in the Christmas issue - the solutions are given in the same issue.

It's the rich mix of fiction, though, that's of most interest to writers, and fiction is what this magazine is all about. There are 14 or 15 stories in each issue. The stories are categorised under descriptive headings: 'Tale with a Twist', 'Put Your Feet Up', 'One from the Heart', 'Spine Chiller', or simply 'Love Story' – with an occasional variant like 'Kidnap Drama'. Story lengths vary considerably. Over the two issues we reviewed, the shortest story was about 800 words, and the longest ran to more than 4,000 words. There's nothing stereotyped or predictable about *Fiction Feast*. More or less anything goes. The policy seems to be to let the stories run to their logical length. Make no mistake, though – these are all well-written, well-structured stories carefully selected to appeal to a wide readership.

All the stories we saw were complete – *Fiction Feast* does not appear to be interested in serials. Some of the stories are undoubtedly agency-sourced, but there is nothing in the magazine to suggest that unsolicited stories won't be read. Remember the s.a.e.

Read a few issues to get the 'feel' of the magazine – it offers an interesting blend of stories that should excite writers of short fiction and stimulate their imagination. *Take a Break's Fiction Feast* deserves to be around for a long and healthy life.

THAT'S LIFE!

Editor: Christabel Smith

Features Editor: Dawn Smith

Fiction Editor: Emma Fabian

H. Bauer Publishing, 3rd Floor, Academic House, 24-28 Oval Road, London NW1 7DT.

Tel: 020 7241 8000. Fax: 020 7241 8008.

Weekly, 60p. Founded 1995. Circulation d. Publishes non-fiction and short fiction. Pay band D, at the end of the month of publication.

A bright and breezy women's magazine from the Bauer stable, *that's life!* is aimed at a broad cross-section, from teenagers to grannies – but more directly at the 20- to 35-year-old woman. A typical issue will consist of 48 colourful saddle-stitched pages of which no more than half a dozen will be advertisements – mostly for videos, mail-order catalogues and the like.

Living up to its title, *that's life!* features a lot of the universally popular True Life stories: five or six one-and-a-half-page 1,000-word stories (£400), a two-page spread of three or four 'It happened to me' 500-worders (£200), and 'My true secret', 800 words (£200). *A major warning though*: these really are true stories and include photographs of the people involved (although names might be changed). Unless you lead a complex life, there's little scope for 'ordinary' freelance writers to write their own stories. Most of the True Life stories, however, are bylined 'As told to ...' and are probably written by a commissioned writer working with the story's subject – there's a form in the magazine inviting readers to send in a brief outline of their story.

As well as the personal experience stories, *that's life!* has a number of regular features: fashion, health, beauty-care, cooking, home decoration and furnishing, readers' problems – and, of course, an astrology column. The magazine also features a considerable number of competitions – word searches, crosswords and space-fillers – all good for reader-participation.

There is also a well-paid regular one-page 750-word 'sting-in-the-tail' short-short story. (They pay £300 each!)

It is, though, its letters and 'fillers' spots that make *that's life!* particularly attractive to the freelance. It's best to study these carefully and frequently before submitting – they emphasise the need for originality and exclusivity. There are regular spots (numbers per week based on sampled issues only – these will obviously vary) for:

- 'Aren't men daft': 40-80 words, 7 items, £25 each, £50 for 'Soft lad of the week'.
- 'Kids are us!': Mums' tips, tales and special moments, 700 words, £250.
- 'Look who's talking': Cute pictures of kids, with captions 15-40 words, £25.
- 'Tightwad tips': 15-30 words, 5 tips, £20 each, £50 with an illustrative photo.
- 'Rude jokes': Lengths vary, 5 jokes, £15 each.
- 'That's your life!' Letters, most not back-issue-related: 50-110 words, 6 letters, £20 each (£50 for the best) plus £5 each for photographs.
- 'It's a rip-off': Sorting out scams and unfair treatment, 300 words, £200.
- 'Moaner of the week': One per week, 45-50 words, £25.

Tip: Keep studying *that's life!* – like all good magazines, it evolves and changes and is never static – or boring.

THE THIRD ALTERNATIVE

Science fiction, fantasy, horror

Editor: Andy Cox, TTA Press, 5 Martin's Lane, Witcham, Ely, Cambs CB6 2LB.

E-mail: ttapress@aol.com Website: www.ttapress.com

Quarterly, £3.75. Founded 1993. Publishes non-fiction and fiction. Query required for non-fiction – *see below*. Pay band A, on publication.

The Third Alternative is one of Britain's most original fiction magazines: it publishes 'an exciting mix of extraordinary new fiction, stunning artwork, in-depth reviews and interviews, fascinating cinema features and provocative comment columns.'

Now supported financially by the Eastern Arts Board and the Arts Council of England, *The Third Alternative* is a fine example of how a small, independent press magazine can grow into the publishing mainstream – without sacrificing its principles. It publishes modern, character-led horror, fantasy and science fiction ... and borderline, 'between-genre' material – they call it 'slipstream'. Its readership is international.

A typical issue of *The Third Alternative* will have 68 much-illustrated saddle-stitched pages – the internal pages are illustrated in black-and-white, the cover in colour. There are only about four pages in all of advertisements, from mainstream (HarperCollins, Orbit) and other publishers.

Editorially, the magazine carries several regular columns – including commentary from Britain and the US – and a substantial Review section focused on books in the magazine's area of interest. The bulk of *The Third Alternative* is devoted to short stories, articles and interviews.

The short stories are largely within the horror, fantasy and science fiction genres – or not too far removed from these (i.e. 'slipstream'). They are often by well-known or up-and-coming authors – and sometimes by first-timers. There are no length restrictions, within reason. The stories can best be described – other than 'new wave' or 'modern' – as uninhibited. In their field, the stories are excellent, and many have won prestigious awards and been reprinted in relevant anthologies.

Submit just one unsolicited story at a time (plus s.a.e., of course). Post your ms flat or one fold only. No reprints or simultaneous submissions.

Submission guidelines for fiction are printed in the magazine.

On the non-fiction side, *The Third Alternative* publishes interviews with relevant authors: Christopher Priest, Peter Straub, Steve Aylett ... but not John Grisham or Danielle Steel. The magazine also uses profiles of influential film-makers. Articles should be around 4,000 words long, plus photos where appropriate. Ideas for other articles – comment, humour, etc. – are also welcomed.

For all non-fiction, query first with a brief outline.

Tip: Whatever you do, study the magazine before submitting anything – *Woman's Weekly* it is not!

THIS ENGLAND

Britain's patriotic quarterly

Editor: Roy Faiers

PO Box 52, Cheltenham, Gloucestershire GL50 1YQ.

Tel: 01242 537900. E-mail: editor@thisengland.co.uk

Website: www.thisengland.co.uk

Quarterly, £4.00. Founded 1968. Circulation figures not known, but 'read by two million patriots all over the world'. Publishes non-fiction and poetry. *Don't send short stories*. Pay band A, at the end of the month of publication.

This England is a glossy quarterly devoted to the glories of the English heritage. It is strong on nostalgia and beautiful, but always traditional, things. (A picture of an old stone bridge, for instance, would almost certainly – and understandably – be more acceptable than one of a slim modern steel-and-concrete one.) The magazine uses a lot of pictures, mostly nowadays in colour, with black-and-white pictures mainly of historical origin. The target readership of *This England* is middle-aged or older, of both sexes, and probably reasonably affluent and well educated.

A typical issue of *This England* will consist of 80-plus lavishly illustrated perfect-bound pages of which only half-a-dozen or so will be advertisements; it is the magazine's publishing policy that 'advertisements should provide a service to readers rather than dominate the magazine'. The advertisements are either classified small ads for everything from vanity book publishers to holiday accommodation, or display advertisements mainly for the magazine's other products, publications, etc.

Editorially, *This England* will contain a number of features forming parts of continuing series such as English country churches, English inns and signs, Christian England, English heroes and the like. There's an interesting twice-yearly feature (in the spring and autumn issues) called 'Parlour Poetry', where readers answer requests from other readers for details of half-forgotten, half-remembered verse.

There are also two regular long-standing sections of the magazine, 'Cornucopia' and 'Forget Me Nots', which offer good opportunities for the freelance writer.

'Cornucopia' uses fifteen or so short (up-to-date) pieces per issue on 'Customs, curiosities and coming events', ranging in length from 200 to 500 words and usually colour-illustrated. Topics in one issue we reviewed included, among others, 'Shrewsbury's hero of the high seas, Admiral John Benbow'; 'Historic origins of horse brasses'; a 'Centennial tribute to submariners'; 24 years of the Knitting and Crochet Guild; the first portrait of Churchill; 'Passing through history at Tixall Gatehouse' and how knots are associated with magical powers.

There are three or four 'Forget Me Nots' in each issue. These are longer pieces, 600-800 words each and pure nostalgia: 'When Valentine came to call ...'; 'The Village Petrol Station'; 'Where Peaceful Waters Flow' (the River Wye in the Welsh border country in 1941); 'My Fourpenny Jesus' (a life-long precious possession). Some of these pieces are illustrated by the staff artist, others with colour or old black-and-white photographs.

There are also many opportunities for longer one-off features in *This England*, such as the 'Great Britons' series and 'Stars of Yesterday' (one issue we read featured Ronald Colman). The same issue included a feature titled 'The River Severn from Source to Sea'. Such features should not normally exceed 2,000 words and are usually profusely illustrated in colour.

This England has a big 'Post Box' (no payment or prizes) using between 40 and 50 letters per issue, many back-issue-related, on topics ranging from well dressing in Nottinghamshire to war brides to flag flying in New Zealand – letters come from all over the world.

This England also uses a lot of poetry, often as page-end fillers. The editor says that short poems (about a dozen lines long) stand the best chance and that poems should be meaningful rather than 'clever'. The poems are noticeably traditional in form, too, invariably having metre and rhyme. Don't submit more than three poems at a time.

If you are a writer-photographer, *This England* offers even more opportunities: they use a lot of free-standing pictures – almost all, now, in colour – either as two-page spreads or as captioned snippets. The big spreads are mainly out-door scenes and preferably include one or more persons *doing* something; the smaller pictures are often of an interesting building, statue or artefact. Preferred subjects include town, country and village scenes, craftsmen at work, curiosities, nostalgia and patriotism. Avoid anything obviously modern.

Colour photos must be transparencies and the Editor prefers them to be 2¼ inches square (120 film) or larger. When black-and-white prints are appropriate, captions and the photographer's name and address should be on the back.

Editorial rejections can be quick – in about a month. Decisions on marginal material often take considerably longer – up to three months. The Editor particularly advises writers NOT to enquire about the fate of their submissions in less than three months. He says, 'Material is invariably returned without further consideration to an over-zealous contributor.'

Contributors are also cautioned to submit seasonal material at least five months before the appropriate publication date – be sure to mention the relevance of the date.

And at the same address:

EVERGREEN
Britain's famous little green quarterly

Editor: Roy Faiers.

Quarterly, £3.25. Founded 1985. Circulation b. Publishes non-fiction and poetry. *Don't send short stories.* Pay band A, at the end of the month of publication.

Evergreen is *This England*'s sister publication, a pocket-sized quarterly of about 150 perfect-bound pages produced by the same editorial team. Its needs and policies are much the same as those of *This England* – but it uses material relevant to Scotland and Wales *as well as* England.

Evergreen describes itself as 'A Miscellany of This and That & Things Gone By' and a 'companion for all who treasure our country's character and traditions'.

Like *This England*, *Evergreen* welcomes unsolicited submissions about towns and villages, and stories of popular music stars of long ago - all similarly old-fashioned, nostalgic and reflective. All the above comments about *This England* are equally relevant to *Evergreen*. All material submitted for *This England* is automatically considered for possible use in *Evergreen* – and vice versa.

And remember – don't chase the editor in less than three months (and even then, only very 'gently'). If you do, your work is rejected.

WANDERLUST

Editorial Director: Lyn Hughes

Wanderlust Magazine, PO Box 1832, Windsor, Berkshire SL4 1YT.

Tel: 01753 620426. Fax: 01753 620474.

E-mail: info@wanderlust.co.uk   Website: www.wanderlust.co.uk

Every two months, £3.50. Founded 1993. Circulation a. Non-fiction only. Query essential except for 'Travellers Tales' – see below. *Don't send short stories or poetry.* Pay band D, within 30 days of submission of invoice after publication.

Wanderlust is a beautifully produced magazine, a pleasure to handle, a joy to read, and an inspiration for everyone interested in travelling. (It's a feast for the armchair traveller, too.) *Wanderlust* aims 'to provide our readers with the best writing, the best photographs and the most authoritative facts ...'

A typical issue of *Wanderlust* will have 138 perfect-bound pages, profusely illustrated with exceptionally fine photographs. About 20 per cent of the pages carry advertisements, for every imaginable kind of travel-related product from safaris to sleeping bags, from luxury cruises to health care insurance.

Wanderlust has news from the world of travel, health care and travel tips, tour news, book and music reviews, lists of thing to do (Going Out or Staying In), product trials, a 'Poste Restante' letters section with prizes for all letters published and a special prize for the best in each issue. There's a selection of readers' travel tips called 'The Knowledge', with a prize for every entry published. And there are prize competitions, including travel writing and the Travel Photo of the Year awards where the winner of each of three categories wins a valuable photographic commission.

Wanderlust regularly includes five types of feature:

Destination features – usually 3 per issue, covering a specific country or region; both anecdotal and informative, with a 'Footnotes' fact page (mostly provided by the writer). Length from 1,800 to 2,200 words. In the issues we reviewed, destinations covered included Louisiana, Sabah (in northern Borneo), Tenerife, Los Roques Caribbean archipelago, and São Tomé in West Africa. *Query essential.*

Ad Hoc features – on the arts, culture, food and wine, issues, investigative pieces etc. Length from 500 to 1,500 words. There's a selection in each issue. *Query essential.*

Travellers' Tales – short anecdotal snapshots or observations, about 300 to 700 words – longer pieces occasionally accepted. Two or three per issue. *Don't query – send the complete piece.*

Special Interest features – authoritative pieces written from in-depth knowledge and experience, 2,000 to 3,000 words. Two or three per issue. *Query essential.*

City Guides – a descriptive introduction followed by a two-page up-to-date factual guide. Around 2,000 words. One or two per issue. *Detailed proposal essential.*

For detailed guidelines (for writers and photographers) send an s.a.e. or look on the website. It's absolutely essential to read these carefully and study several issues of the magazine before offering anything. 'It's no coincidence that most of *Wanderlust*'s contributors are regular readers.' Give it your very best – it's a great magazine.

Tip: Wanderlust does not use fiction, but fiction writers would find it an inspirational and reliable source of information on exotic locations.

THE WEEKLY NEWS

Editor: David Burness

D. C. Thomson & Co Ltd, Albert Square, Dundee, Scotland DD1 9QJ.

Tel: 01382 223131. Fax: 01382 201390. E-mail: weeklynews@dcthomson.co.uk

Website: www.dcthomson.co.uk

Weekly, 50p. Founded 1855. Circulation c. Non-fiction and cartoons. *Don't send short stories or poetry.* Pay band C, on acceptance.

The Weekly News is a tabloid-sized weekly newspaper aimed at the TV-quiz-game and Coronation Street viewer. The paper is designed to appeal mainly to busy housewives and working mothers, although many men enjoy it too – the content includes regular pages featuring sporting news and personalities.

A typical issue of *The Weekly News* will have 30-plus 'newspaper-style' pages, much illustrated in both colour and black-and-white. Spread throughout these pages will be the equivalent of about 4 pages of advertisements, for mail-order goods, health products, and other DCT publications.

Editorially, there are several pages of news – including 'Telly Talk: to help you enjoy the best on the box', 'Inside Hollywood – stars, gossip and reviews' – and a number of regular columns. The regulars include 'best buys', health and life-style, fashion, a page of puzzles and jokes, gardening, travel, DIY, and sports ... and many cartoons. There are also many reader offers and prize competitions.

Most issues of *The Weekly News* feature one or two readers' own stories told in the first person – but not necessarily written by the actual protagonist. In one issue we read, a feature told how a mother was inadvertently poisoning her son by giving him food to which he was allergic, bylined 'As told to ...' The same issue had the story of how a mother coped with her daughter's suffering from the extremely rare condition 'Selective Mutism'. The paper welcomes such stories, up to 1,500 words.

The Editor is particularly interested in celebrity interviews/profiles – and not necessarily only of top stars. Features on the royals are also welcome. One issue we reviewed included an extract from June Whitfield's autobiography, a short feature about Johnny Ball, and a piece on *Heartbeat* star Tricia Penrose's ambitions to be a pop star. In the same issue there were several short (200-500 words) general-interest pieces, for example, 'Homework on the web': how new technology is helping children cope with homework; 'Adopt a Beaver': about the Mammals Trust UK; and the search for a more apt descriptive term than 'senior citizens' for the over-sixties.

There are 'filler' opportunities in:

• The Letters page – about a dozen letters each week. Not usually back-issue-related, often amusing/embarrassing, about 50-100 words long; £10 for the best, a prize of a pen for the rest.

• 'Readers' Top Tips' – Time and/or money-saving tips. They use 3 or 4 each week, 20-50 words long, the main Top Tip winning £10, the others £5.

All letters, etc., should be marked appropriately and addressed to The Weekly News, 185 Fleet Street, London EC4A 2HS. Other material, i.e., short features or news items, can be faxed or sent by post to Dundee (above), although potential contributors should be warned that 90% of copy is produced in-house each week.

WOMAN

Editor: Carole Russell

IPC Media Ltd, King's Reach Tower, Stamford Street, London SE1 9LS.

Tel: 020 7261 7023. Fax: 020 7261 5947. E-mail: woman@ipcmedia.com

Weekly, 68p. Founded 1937. Circulation d. Publishes non-fiction and short fiction (*but see below*). Pay band D, at the end of the month of publication.

Woman is a bright and breezy weekly designed to be a 'good quick read'. Its target readership is all 'mid-market' (i.e., not short of a bob or two but not seriously affluent) women, from teenagers to grannies – but its core readership is women of 20 to 40, with children.

A typical issue of *Woman* will have 60 colourful saddle-stitched pages of which 9 or 10 will be advertisements – for a range of products from food to cosmetics, from pharmaceutical products to laundry aids. There are also usually several special reader offers.

Editorially, there are many regular sections: fashion, beauty-care, health and cookery. There are two pages of news about the soaps, their stars, and other celebrities. There is an astrology column and several problem-answer pages.

Like so many other magazines, *Woman* includes several Real Life stories in each issue, offering readers up to £300 for such stories; instructions on how to contact them about your story are given in the magazine, and include a special 'Story hotline' phone number. These are genuine stories which 'must be true and authentic' and the person offering their story must be prepared to be photographed. Most of these stories are assigned to experienced writers.

Woman also publishes features from freelance writers. If you have previously had features published in similar magazines and happened to hear of a really interesting woman's experience or way of life, you might try querying the Features Editor. In issues we reviewed, there were features about a woman who walked out on a 22-year marriage to be with a man she met through an internet chat room; another told of a woman whose parents both died in the same week she became engaged to be married. In the same issues, there were interviews with Britney Spears and Peter Davison; if you're in a position to secure a celebrity interview, it would certainly be worth a query.

The magazine carries a one-page short-short story each week. Many of these are agency-supplied, but they'll consider really good, *suitable* stories of up to 1,000 words. *Woman* short stories are more literary than most of the fiction currently being published in weekly magazines. Carefully study as many published *Woman* stories as you can before submitting. But be warned – they state in tiny print near the back of the magazine that they 'do not accept or return unsolicited manuscripts', so they'll probably only get back to you if they're really interested.

There is a lively Letters page in *Woman* (write to 'You tell us'), using about 9 or 10 short (40-100 words) letters each week. Letters earn £15 each plus £5 for associated photographs, and the best of the week gets £25.

WOMAN ALIVE

Editor: Liz Trundle

Christian Media Centre Ltd, Garcia Estate, Canterbury Road, Worthing, West Sussex BN13 1EH.

Tel: 01903 821082. Fax: 01903 821081.

E-mail: womanalive@christianmedia.org.uk

Monthly, £1.90. Circulation a. Publishes non-fiction only. *Don't send poetry or short stories.* Pay band B, at the end of the month of publication.

Woman Alive is Britain's only Christian magazine aimed at women. It covers all denominations and deals with issues relevant to active Christians as well as general interest features, celebrity profiles, health etc. It is written for women of all ages – married, single, divorced or widowed – but particularly the 25-45 age group.

Woman Alive is a very readable magazine. Although Christian values and beliefs are apparent on every page, it does not *inappropriately* preach. Unless you are a committed Christian, though, there is little point in submitting material or ideas, as the Editor asks for a brief biography – Christian (and writing) background – from all new writers. (She also asks for samples of published work, but if you have none, try anyway.)

A typical issue of *Woman Alive* will consist of 48 profusely and colourfully illustrated saddle-stitched pages of which about a quarter are advertisements, for religious books, CDs, holidays, charities, and jobs. There are also reader offers and competitions.

On the editorial side there are regular (commissioned or staff-written) features on contemporary issues, on health and on relationships; there are book and film reviews, and a round-up of news from churches and charities in the UK and abroad. There are also several one-off freelance-contributed features, 9 or 10 in each issue: some, like the 1,000-word celebrity interviews, are usually commissioned, others are 'writer-initiated'.

In the two issues we reviewed, one interview was with Premier League hockey player Jill Ireland, who talked about her twin passions, Jesus and sport; another featured Fran Beckett, CEO of the Shaftesbury Society and Chair of Rebuild, a woman with a passion to change communities for the better.

Among the other features in these issues were: 'Mind, body and spirit: How to keep the balance'; a feature on a woman who began a modelling career in her eighties; an exposé of male 'dictatorship' within the Church; and 'Organic – Hype or Healthy?: Farming and the food we eat'.

All these features, and the several others in these issues, were illustrated with colour photographs.

The back page has a regular feature, 'Manalive', written by a man – in one of these features the writer asked, 'Should the Church be above branding itself for the sake of PR?'; in another, a man who had taken on the school run found, through conversations at the school gates, that 'more and more highly intelligent women are turning to psychics for spiritual guidance'. These features were illustrated with appropriate colour artwork.

Tip: It's best to approach the Editor with ideas in the first instance.

WOMAN & HOME

Editorial Director: Sue James

PA: Sandra Kearns

IPC Media Ltd, King's Reach Tower, Stamford Street, London SE1 9LS.

Tel: 020 7261 5176.

Monthly, £2.60. Founded 1926. Circulation c. Publishes non-fiction and short fiction (*but see below*). Pay band D, at the end of the month of publication.

Woman & Home is an upmarket monthly magazine aimed at women of 35-plus, relatively affluent, intelligent, pleasantly house-proud and in a stable family relationship. They may or may not be women who work outside the home.

A typical issue of *Woman & Home* will have about 160 much-illustrated perfectbound pages, of which nearly a third will be advertisements. The adverts are mainly for clothes, cosmetic and pharmaceutical products, holidays (cruises and the like) and 'interesting' foodstuffs.

Within the editorial pages, each issue of *Woman & Home* will have regular sections/departments covering homes and gardens, fashion and beauty, health and fitness, cooking, product-testing and travel. There are regular pages featuring special offers, giveaways, horoscopes, and offering advice. There is a small, non-paying Letters page, using mostly back-issue-related letters and giving one prize to the best letter of the month.

There are several one-off features and a short story in every issue. But ... in small print in a panel on a page near the end of the magazine, headed 'Reader information', they say:

'We never accept unsolicited manuscripts or pictures, including fiction, and if submitted, we cannot return them.'

So ... don't send anything on spec. And certainly don't bother them at all (see below) if you're not already well experienced.

However, some of the one-off material in the magazine is undoubtedly freelancesupplied. A few features we saw which could – potentially – have been writerinitiated and then commissioned from freelance writers included: 'An affair ... without sex – how a friendly flirtation had devastating emotional consequences for one woman'; 'Simplify your life – How to rediscover what and who is important in your life'; and 'Whose home is it anyway' – a look at the problems of sharing our homes with grownup children. The same issue featured an interview with radio DJ and 'Home Truths' presenter John Peel; if you can offer a celebrity interview you might stand a good chance of breaking in. And even their 'stable' of proven reliable freelances had to start somewhere.

If you have a really *relevant* idea for a *Woman & Home* feature, send them a *brief* outline in writing, by post, plus one or two photocopied sheets of similar published work. If they like the idea, they'll get back to you – if not, they won't.

If – *and only if* – you're a well published, fairly 'literary', and/or well-known shortstory writer, and not yet on *Woman & Home*'s 'list', it might be worth asking whether you can send them a story or two. Otherwise, try entering their short story competition.

WOMAN'S OWN

Editor: Elsa McAlonan

IPC Connect Ltd, King's Reach Tower, Stamford Street, London SE1 9LS.

Tel (features desk): 0870 123 4225. Fax: 020 7261 5346.

E-mail (features): featuresown@ipc.co.uk

Website: www.ipcmedia.com

Weekly, 68p. Founded 1932. Circulation d. Publishes non-fiction (Real Life stories) and fiction, *but does not accept unsolicited material – see below.* Pay band D, at the end of the month of publication.

Woman's Own is the sister magazine of IPC's *Woman* (see page 82) and is similarly bright and cheerful. Like *Woman,* its target readership is all 'mid-market' women, from teenagers to grannies, but its core readership is perhaps slightly older – say 30- to 45-year-olds.

A typical issue of *Woman's Own* has 60 colourful saddle-stitched pages of which about a dozen are advertisements – mainly for food, home-making goods, and cosmetic and pharmaceutical products. There are also special reader offers – one we saw was for a tricolour hibiscus, and, in another issue, a stylish handbag.

On the editorial side there are several regular sections: fashion, health and fitness, beauty-care, cooking, home-making, money and travel. There is an astrology column, several problem-answer pages, and a 'Celebrity' section: each issue has a 'Big interview' – one we saw was with Richard Gere, another featured 'Hornblower' star Ioan Gruffudd – and there's a regular spot titled 'A minute with ...' the likes of Jenny Agutter and James Gaddas.

Each issue of *Woman's Own* has several Real Life stories, and readers are invited to call if they can offer one. These, of course, are true stories, but they're bylined to writers other than the subjects of the stories, so they're probably either staff-written or commissioned from regular feature-writers.

There are no obvious opportunities for 'ordinary' freelance article-writers, but if you have already had material – features or short fiction – published in similar magazines, and have an idea for a really *relevant* article or story, it would be worth querying the Editor. Make it a *short* query letter and send only photocopies of previously published work, plus an s.a.e. – you might not get them back, though, nor even a reply. In tiny print on an inside page the magazine states: 'We regret that we cannot ... answer any letters or return submitted material unless accompanied by an SAE. We also regret that we cannot accept unsolicited fiction manuscripts.' That's quite clear, and fair enough.

There is a regular short-short story spot, 'Quick Read' – but here again the magazine does not welcome unsolicited submissions. The stories used in this spot appear to be either written by 'name' authors or sourced from agencies.

Among the regular columns there is, of course, a Letters page. This uses 8 or 9 letters each week, some as long as 100 words, and some are back-issue-related. Published letters earn £20 each with £50 for the best each week. They also offer £25 for the 'Picture of the Week'. Photographs are not returned.

WOMAN'S WEEKLY

Editor: Gilly Sinclair

Fiction Editor: Gaynor Davies

IPC Connect Ltd, King's Reach Tower, Stamford Street, London SE1 9LS.

Tel: 0870 444 5000.

Weekly, 66p. Founded 1911. Circulation d. Publishes non-fiction and fiction. Pay band D, at the end of the month of publication.

Woman's Weekly, which now incorporates *Woman's Realm*, is still going strong after more than 90 years, increasing its circulation despite aggressive competition from newer brands in the women's magazine market. It has modernised itself, and is no longer the purple-and-pink-covered journal of 'royalty, romance and recipes' (the old well tried formula), although there are still lots of good recipes and fiction. The readership of *Woman's Weekly* nowadays is a broader church – but with the emphasis slightly on the more mature woman of 35-plus years.

A typical issue of the magazine will have about 68 colourful saddle-stitched pages of which about twenty per cent will be advertisements – for clothes, health products, stair lifts, life insurance policies and the like. There are always plenty of special offers, and prize crossword competitions.

On the editorial side there are many regular sections: always several pages of scrumptious-sounding recipes, and a section containing a knitting or other pattern. There are regular pages covering gardening, travel, fashion, health, home-craft and parenthood; a 'Between Friends' column by Canon Roger Royle; a 'Wit and Wisdom' column from Terry Wogan; and of course, there are astrology and 'agony' columns.

There are one-off feature articles, too, but it would be unwise to submit anything on spec – query your idea first; most of the opportunities seem to be 'celebrity-associated'; one issue we reviewed featured actress Judy Loe 'on the couch'.

The *Woman's Weekly* Letters page is a good opening for writers that way inclined; they use ten or so letters (more or less any length, 30-100 words), paying £10 each with £25 for the best of the week, there's also a spot paying £10 for a 'Celebrations' letter plus accompanying photograph, and a £15 prize for one funny photo each week.

But it is for its fiction that writers (and readers, of course) are most interested in *Woman's Weekly*. The popularity of the fiction is proved by the success of sister publication *Woman's Weekly Fiction Special* (see next page). There is always a serial and two or three short stories in each issue. 'Coffee-break read' is a short-short of about 1,000 words.

The other stories are of any length from 1,000 to 3,000 words, and should have believable, *up-to-date* characters in modern, believable situations, an unpredictable storyline, an element of tension or conflict, and possibly, but not necessarily, an element of romance. *No* explicit sex or violence, sci-fi, ghost, or nostalgia. Stories can be about children, teenagers, family problems, humorous, crime or thriller (not threatening or violent). Aim for stories with a warm quality.

WOMAN'S WEEKLY FICTION SPECIAL

Editor: Olwen Rice

Fiction Editor: Gaynor Davies

IPC Connect Ltd, King's Reach Tower, Stamford Street, London SE1 9LS.

Tel: 020 7261 5000.

Every other month, £1.30. Founded 1998. Circulation c. Publishes short fiction and mini-serials. Pay band D, on publication.

Woman's Weekly Fiction Special has proved so popular it now appears regularly every other month. The magazine is totally devoted to fiction, other than a few pages of puzzles and a regular feature on a well-known author like Ruth Rendell or Josephine Cox, who share their writing secrets with readers.

A typical issue of *Woman's Weekly Fiction Special* will have about 76 A4 pages packed with great fiction. There are only a few pages of display ads, mainly for novels.

There are always several stories by 'name' authors - Frederick Forsyth, Charlotte Bingham, Marian Keyes, Maeve Binchy, Andrea Newman, Sheila O'Flanagan and Gwen Moffat have all featured recently – but all the other stories (about 20 per issue) are freelance-contributed. You'll probably recognise, as I do, many regular contributors to *Woman's Weekly* itself; the stories in the *Specials* are of the same high standard and particular philosophy as the weekly magazine: the Editor looks for stories which portray up-to-date characters in believable, modern situations; problems, funny stories and even stories with a crime or thriller element, so long as they are not violent, threatening or too incredible. In other words, 'fiction that grips readers and stirs their emotions rather than sending them to sleep!' The 'shout lines' on the covers of two *Specials* we reviewed promised 'terrific stories of love ... and betrayal' and 'gripping tales you cannot miss'.

Like *Woman's Weekly*, the *Fiction Special* imposes a few caveats: the stories must not depict explicit sex or violence; the main characters, while living firmly in the present, must be basically decent caring people. Depressing stories are out. Ideally, stories should have a warm quality and if possible a happy or at least a satisfying ending to make readers feel uplifted and hopeful. Crime stories need not have happy endings as such but justice must be seen to have been done.

'Twist in the tale' stories should be 1,000 words, other stories can be any length from 1,000 to 8,000 words.

All manuscripts must be typewritten in double spacing with good margins. And don't forget the essential s.a.e.

WRITERS' FORUM

Incorporating World Wide Writers

Editor: John Jenkins

Deputy Editor: Mary Hogarth

Poetry Editor: Morgan Kenney

PO Box 3229, Bournemouth BH1 1ZS.

Tel: 01202 589828. Fax: 01202 587758. E-mail: writintl@globalnet.co.uk

Ten a year, £3.00 (from newsagents and on subscription – details from the above address). Circulation a. Publishes non-fiction, fiction (*but only from their own competitions – see below*), poetry, writing-related cartoons. Query advisable for features. Pay band C, at the end of the month *after* the month of publication.

Part of Writers International Ltd, *Writers' Forum* is 'dedicated to providing encouragement and inspiration to those who want to write and see their work published'. *Writers' Forum* has now been amalgamated with sister publication *World Wide Writers*, and now includes the short story and poetry competitions previously featured in that magazine.

There is also a lively Letters page, mainly back-issue-related. The Editor welcomes letters on all topics connected with writing.

Writers' Forum is an attractively produced publication, typically with 76 colourfully illustrated saddle-stitched pages. The advertisements it carries are mainly, as you would expect, for services to writers, writers' events, writing courses and the like.

Editorially, the magazine offers a mix of features advising its readership on all aspects of writing from getting started to publishing in print and on the internet. In the issues we reviewed, readers were advised on: writing scripts; writing comedy; putting your books on tape to reach a wider audience; the art of biography; writing crime fiction; dealing with rejection; thinking about beginnings and endings in short story-writing; researching for 'star' interviews; editing your own work; writing a successful novel ... plus market information - plenty of advice and encouragement for both aspiring and established writers.

Writers' Forum welcomes submissions as follows:

- Non-fiction (writing-related material only, especially biography), length 500-1,500 words, but *please* send a query letter first, in case your topic has already been covered, payment £80 per 1,000 words. Interviews with established writers are particularly welcome.

- Poetry, maximum length 42 lines, payment £20 per poem.

- Cartoons and other illustrations relevant to writing, payment by arrangement.

Writers' Forum now includes the competitions previously run by *World Wide Writers*, and offers substantial prizes plus publication for winning stories – entry forms and details of fees and prizes are in the magazine.

The Editor advises: 'Please do not submit anything unless you have read the publication.'

WRITERS' NEWS

Editor: Derek Hudson

Yorkshire Post Newspapers Ltd, PO Box 168, Wellington Street, Leeds LS1 1RF.

Tel: 0113 238 8333.

Fax: 0113 238 8330.

Website: www.writersnews.co.uk

Monthly, subscription only: £39.90 UK, £44.90 RoW. Founded 1989. Publishes non-fiction – all writing-related – and short fiction, but the latter *only* from its own competitions. Pay band C, at the end of the month of publication.

Writers' News, founded by David St. John Thomas, was bought by Yorkshire Post Newspapers Ltd in 2000. The new owners continue to foster the concept that subscribers are *members of a club*. It also emphasises the news element of its title: each issue contains a dozen or more pages of news items, all writing-related.

Subscribers to *Writers' News* also receive, included in the subscription (see above), each year's six bi-monthly issues of *Writing Magazine* (see next page). In the months when *Writing Magazine* appears, *Writers' News* contains around 32 pages – about 50% news, 20% advertisements, and the rest, a few of the regular columns. Nearly all the expected regulars and features are in *Writing Magazine* in those months.

In the alternate months, when 'on its own', *Writers' News* has 64 pages: a dozen or so are news, a similar number carry adverts … and there are many regular columns/ pages/sections – including a lively Letters page which gives a £20 book voucher for the monthly Star Letter. Other regulars include a 2- to 3-page interview with a leading author, a 2- to 3-page market review (usually in batches of related-subject magazines), sections on children's books, technology, writing style and practice, and a couple of chatty columns, one by the former publisher (who maintains a keen interest in the business) and one from the editorial side. There are regular poetry 'workshops', critical reviews of the magazine's prize-winning short stories, and a problems page.

Listing the regulars exemplifies the overall 'feel' of the magazine: there are very few one-off articles by other than the regular writers. (That doesn't necessarily mean that if you have an idea for a one-off article or short series, *Writers' News* wouldn't be interested – just that such one-offs are few and far between.) All features – regular columns, series or one-offs – are by experts. This is no place to try to 'break your duck'.

The target readership of *Writers' News* is, of course, all writers – and any writer will find much of interest in it. But it tends to aim more at the struggling beginner than at the successful writer. Its editorial attitude tends to encourage – in our view, perhaps over-enthusiastically – the idea of self-publishing; although, of course, it speaks out against vanity publishing.

Decisions tend to come quickly – in less than a month – and outlines are preferred to complete articles. *Writers' News* also welcomes news items – including 'your own news', so don't be bashful.

WRITING MAGAZINE

Editor: Derek Hudson

Yorkshire Post Newspapers Ltd, PO Box 168, Leeds LS1 1RF.

Tel: 0113 238 8333. Fax: 0113 238 8330.

E-mail: derek.hudson@writersnews.co.uk

Bi-monthly, £3.00 – free to *Writers' News* subscribers. Founded 1992. Publishes non-fiction (all writing-related) and short fiction (*but only from their own competitions*). Pay band C, at the end of the month of publication.

Launched in 1992 as a quarterly news-stand partner to the by then well established *Writers' News* (see previous page), *Writing Magazine* is supplied free to *Writers' News* subscribers. Now a bi-monthly, each issue contains all the regular columns that would otherwise have been in that month's issue of *Writers' News* – plus several more.

A typical issue of *Writing Magazine* contains about 64 A4 saddle-stitched pages of which almost a quarter are advertisements: for *Writers' News* correspondence courses and book club, for tuition and conferences, for writing services – particularly offers of manuscript-vetting by experienced author-editors – and for printers etc. offering to assist those intent on self-publishing. The rest of the magazine consists very largely of regular columns/pages/sections.

Regular features include an excellent 3-page interview of a famous author (by Judith Spelman), plus half a dozen shorter, one-page, sometimes unattributed profiles of other (not necessarily lesser) authors. There are columns and series dealing with research, legal and financial matters, fitness, information technology, screen-writing, poetry, article-writing, various aspects of fiction-writing and writing for children.

There's a column for beginners, a page or so of book reviews, a problems page, and a Letters page using about a dozen letters per issue, the best winning a book voucher. In the course of a typical year, *Writing* covers just about every area of writing and getting published - you name it, there's probably a column about it.

Other than a useful market study article in each issue, usually focusing on one particular area of the magazine market, there is virtually no writing *news* in *Writing Magazine* – all the news is in the associated *Writers' News*. *Writing Magazine* itself always contains one or more writing competitions of its own. The target reader of *Writing Magazine* is slightly harder to define than that of *Writers' News*; clearly all readers are potential writers, but news-stand buyers are perhaps more 'casual' and thus less dedicated than *Writers' News* 'members'. Like *Writers' News*, though, the magazine is clearly aimed at the wannabe rather than the more experienced writer.

There are few opportunities for articles by contributors who are not 'regulars' – but it is possible for an experienced and knowledgeable writer to break in with ideas for one-off articles or short series. One-page articles need to be around 800 words, with longer articles running to a maximum of 1,500 words. The best initial approach is with an outline. Decisions come quickly – in less than a month.

Tip: Writing Magazine is no place to launch your writing career. If you don't have a track record in some aspect of the writing/publishing world, don't waste the Editor's time.

YOURS

Editor-in-Chief: Neil Patrick

Editor: Christine Moss

YOURS, Bushfield House, Orton Centre, Peterborough PE2 5UW.

Tel: 01733 237111. Fax: 01733 288129.

Monthly, £1.10. Founded 1973. Circulation d. Publishes non-fiction, short fiction and poetry. Pay band A, at the end of the month of publication.

YOURS is aimed at lively senior citizens. It is clear from the magazine contents – adverts, questions, friend-tracing services, etc. – that its target readership is pensioners, of both sexes, but nearer their seventieth than their sixtieth birthdays.

A typical issue of *YOURS* has 150-plus saddle-stitched pages, of which almost half are advertisements, for retirement homes, investment opportunities, and for recliner and motor-powered chairs, stair lifts, support footwear and the like.

Editorially, the magazine abounds in regular features: columns on gardening, legal matters, social benefits, beauty care, pets, money matters, health and fitness. There are recipes, patterns, a problem-solving page, a prize crossword and various other prize competitions. 'Show-business' memories and personalities are often featured in *YOURS*. There's a chatty column by Roy Hudd, several celebrity interviews, and many extra supplements. All issues have free pull-out sheet music. There's also advice on using computers and the Internet – *YOURS* keeps its readers up to date.

As well as the regulars and the many staff-written features, there are openings for one-off freelance articles, usually 700-800-word pieces. One we saw told how reading her mother's diaries prompted a reader to put her own memories on paper. Another looked at the oddities in an old-fashioned recipe book. Such pieces are welcomed but will often be put 'on hold' for quite a while before publication. There is also a 'Frankly Speaking' opinion spot, up to 500 words; a payment is offered for these contributions. Each issue has a travel piece: one we read told of a trip to the Alaskan wilderness, with photos of humpback whales and black bears. Don't query in advance – submit complete articles.

There is always a short story (up to 1,700 words, but often shorter) in which at least some, though not all, of the characters are senior citizens. This is a good freelance market, but there's a lot of competition and usually a stack of accepted stories awaiting publication.

YOURS is particularly attractive for its various Letters pages:

- 'Meeting place' uses up to 40 short (and sometimes abbreviated) letters and tips per issue. You'll probably have a better chance if you send a relevant photograph with your letter. The pay is small, £3 each and £10 for the best, but it's a big 'market'. This section includes 'Talkback': readers' comments on recently published letters.
- 'Titbits' is a page of 8 or 9 snippets, from 15 to 150 words, a miscellany of amusing anecdotes, misprints, and reminiscences, paying £3 for each one published.
- 'Readers' poems' prints two or three short poems, each receiving £10.
- 'Leaving you smiling', the last page, prints 15 or 16 'humorous look at life' letters, including 'The things kids say', and pays £3 for each letter published.

There are also *YOURS Specials* four times a year, bumper extra issues which also use letters, short stories and articles. There is also a *YOURS Fiction Special*.

2

WRITING FOR AMERICAN MAGAZINES

There's a great big English-speaking world out there. *The Writers' & Artists' Yearbook* lists Australian, Canadian, New Zealand and South African magazines plus reference sources for American markets open to UK contributors. As well as offering new work, you can resell material already published in the UK *provided you've only sold British rights*.

Listed below are just a few American fiction magazines, to give you an introduction to this huge and lucrative market. The main source of information for US markets is the annual *Writer's Market* published by Writer's Digest Books, who also publish *Writer's Digest Magazine* and *Novel and Short Story Writer's Market*, *Children's Writer's and Illustrator's Market*, and *Poet's Market*. These market guides are readily available in larger branches of Waterstone's. *Writer's Digest* has an excellent website (www.writersdigest.com) where you can read features from the magazine, check out markets, and sign up to receive a regular free e-mail newsletter packed with features and information.

Most American magazines issue comprehensive writers' guidelines as standard practice, both in print form and on their websites. Read these guidelines carefully and follow them – you'll greatly enhance your chances of success. On the websites, too, you can often access and read copies of the magazines you want to target. If you don't have access either to the internet or to a current copy of *Writer's Market*, request guidelines by post, sending a self-addressed envelope and two IRCs. The guidelines give detailed information for potential contributors, including length restrictions, rights required, payment offered, and how they like to be approached.

Remember to enclose a suitably sized self-addressed envelope plus enough IRCs for the return of your work. If your ms is disposable, say so – but you still need to enclose a business size s.a.e. plus two IRCs for their reply. If you prefer, you can buy US stamps on-line at www.usps.com (the site of United States Postal Services), where you can also find current postal rates and other helpful information.

Invest in an American-English dictionary. Many spellings – and even some meanings – are different from the English language as we know it, so write like a pro, in 'American' English. If rights required are not specified, offer 'First North American Rights', which also covers Canada.

The magazines listed below are available in print (as paperback books) and can be found in or ordered through independent newsagents and larger bookshops. Guidelines and subscription details are on the websites.

ASIMOV'S Science Fiction

Editor: Gardner Dozois.

Address: Dell Magazine Fiction Group, 475 Park Avenue South, 11th Floor, New York, NY 10016, USA.

E-mail: asimovs@asimovs.com Website: www.asimovs.com

Guidelines are available by post or online.

11 a year (including one double issue). About £3.50 per issue in the UK. Subscription price from UK: $18.97 for six months. Established 1977. Circulation b. Publishes short fiction and poetry. Pay band D, on acceptance.

Asimov's will consider material submitted by any writer whether previously published or not. Their list of published writers reads like a 'Who's Who?' of science fiction writing – Robert Silverberg, Brian Aldiss, Orson Scott Card, for example – but they say they've bought some their best stories from people who have never sold a story before.

They look for character-oriented fiction, in which the characters are the main focus of interest rather than the science. And there's always room for humour. No 'sword and sorcery' though, or explicit sex or violence.

Length required is 750 to 15,000 words; *Asimov's* seldom buys stories longer than 15,000 words, and they don't serialise novels.

Payment ranges from 5 to 8 cents a word – established writers get more than beginners.

ALFRED HITCHCOCK'S MYSTERY MAGAZINE

Dell Magazines, 475 Park Avenue South, 11th Floor, New York, NY 10016, USA. Website: www.themysteryplace.com

11 a year, subscription $19.97 for 6 months (international price). Circulation d. Publishes crime/mystery short stories only. Pay band D, on acceptance.

All stories must fall into the mystery genre, and can include classic detection, police procedurals, private eye stories, suspense, courtroom dramas, espionage – stories involving a crime or the threat of a crime. Read the magazine and see submission guidelines etc. at the website. Typical authors include Doug Alleyn, Cynthia Lawrence, Mat Coward.

Preferred length is under 14,000 words, and most stories are considerably shorter than that. The magazine uses original unpublished material only, no simultaneous submissions. *No true crime or stories based on true crime cases.*

For a sample copy, send a cheque or money order for $5.00.

Note: Although *Alfred Hitchcock's Mystery Magazine* shares an address with *Ellery Queen's Mystery Magazine* (see below), stories submitted to one magazine are not considered for the other. Submissions must be made separately.

ELLERY QUEEN'S MYSTERY MAGAZINE

Dell Magazines, 475 Park Avenue South, 11ᵗʰ Floor, New York, NY 10016, USA. Website: www.themysteryplace.com

11 a year, subscription $19.97 for 6 months (international price). Founded 1941. Circulation b. Short fiction only. Pay band D, on acceptance.

Submissions are welcome from both new and established writers. The magazine is especially happy to see first stories by writers who have never before published fiction professionally. They ask that such submissions be addressed to '*Ellery Queen's Mystery Magazine*'s Department of First Stories' at the above address.

Ellery Queen's Mystery Magazine uses stories of just about any length, but prefers 2,500 to 8,000 words. Occasionally they will use an exceptionally good story of up to 12,000 words, and they feature one or two short novels – up to 20,000 words – each year, although these slots are usually given to established writers.

They look for strong writing, an original and exciting plot, and professional craftsmanship. The range in the mystery genre is extensive. They will consider almost any story involving crime or the threat of crime. They ask, though, that you read at least one issue before submitting any work. You can get a sample copy by sending $5.00 (cheque or money order). You can see submission guidelines and further details at the website, and read the magazine online.

The magazine does not consider stories previously published in the USA.

THE MAGAZINE OF FANTASY & SCIENCE FICTION

Editor/Publisher: Gordon Van Gelder.

Fantasy & Science Fiction, PO Box 3447, Hoboken, NJ 07030, USA.

Website: www.sfsite.com

11 a year, subscription $39.97 (international price). Circulation b. Publishes non-fiction and fiction – *but see below*. Pay band D, on acceptance.

Fantasy & Science Fiction looks for stories that will appeal to science fiction and fantasy readers. They have no specific formula for fiction, but require an SF element, however slight, in all stories. They prefer character-based stories, and say that, while they receive a lot of fantasy fiction, they never get enough science fiction or humour. They publish fiction up to 25,000 words in length.

Fantasy & Science Fiction publishes such eminent writers as Ray Bradbury, Ursula K Le Guin, Ben Bova and Terry Bisson, but considers stories from both published and unpublished authors. See the website for comprehensive submission guidelines and copies to read online.

A sample copy is available for $5.00 (cheque or money order) from the above address.

Note: Columns and non-fiction articles are all assigned in-house.

ZOETROPE: ALL-STORY

Editor-in-Chief: Adrienne Brodeur

Zoetrope: All-Story, 916 Kearny Street, San Francisco, CA 94133, USA.

Tel: (415) 788 7500.

E-mail (general information): info@all-story.com

E-mail: (submissions information): submissions@all-story.com

Website: www.all-story.com

Quarterly, $40 a year (international price). Founded 1997. Circulation a. Short literary fiction and one-act plays. Pay band D.

Zoetrope: All-Story looks for quality short fiction. Stories are chosen on literary merit – on the voice of the writer, the quality of the writing, the lustre of the characters and the depth of the plot. They look for stories that illuminate contemporary life and the human condition.

The magazine was founded by Francis Ford Coppola and Adrienne Brodeur to stimulate and sustain the story-telling tradition in the form of the quality short story. They are keen to encourage 'the new generation of classic short stories'. The stories they are particularly interested in finding are those that have potential as screenplays – *but they require the stories to be submitted as short stories, NOT screenplays.* They want tightly written stories that have a compelling narrative flow.

Zoetrope: All-Story considers unsolicited short fiction and one-act plays no longer than 7,000 words. Submit only one story or one play at a time. *Excerpts from larger works, screenplays, treatments, and poetry will be return unread.* They will not respond to any submissions sent without a self-addressed envelope, either stamped or accompanied by the appropriate number of IRCs.

The magazine runs an annual short story competition, offering substantial money prizes, up to $1,000.

Zoetrope: All-Story buys First North American Serial Rights and a 2-year film option.

There is also an online 'Virtual Studio' where submissions can be made electronically. *The print magazine does not accept submissions via e-mail.* Membership of the Virtual Studio is free. You can submit your stories by e-mail and get feedback from other writers as well as having your work considered for publication by the *Zoetrope: All-Story* editorial staff.

Note: Zoetrope: All-Story has moved (in 2002) from New York to the above address in California. The address given in the 2002 *Writer's Market* is now out of date.

3

WHO USES WHAT?

It is of course not possible to list, in any precise manner, the stories and articles that will attract the interest of an editor. Editors are always looking for something new – but not too new – something that they haven't done before and that they think will particularly interest their readers. It is one of the tasks of the freelance writer to come up with new ideas that will spark off the Editor's interest. Having said that, there are broad categories of article subjects which fall naturally into the areas of interest of different magazines.

The lists below, broad though the subjects are, offer a general idea of which magazine is most likely to be interested in articles on which subject.

The story market lists categorise magazines generally by story length, differentiating between markets for the increasingly popular 'short-short' story (up to, say, 1,000 words at most) and for the longer story (with about 2,500 words usually being preferred).

ARTICLES – BY SUBJECT

General Interest/Factual/Biography

Active Life

Antiques & Collectables

Autocar

Best of British

Cat World

Choice

Collect it!

Country Life

Country Quest

The Countryman

Eve

Evergreen

The Field

Focus

Geographical

Good Housekeeping

Home & Country

Homes & Gardens

Ireland's Own

The Lady

The People's Friend

Practical Family History

Prospect

The Railway Magazine

Red

Saga Magazine

The Scots Magazine

This England

Yours

The National Heritage/Nostalgia – the Countryside, the Buildings and the Artefacts

Antiques & Collectables

Best of British

Collect it!

Country Life

The Countryman

Country Quest

Country Walking

Evergreen

The Field

Good Housekeeping

Home & Country

Homes & Gardens

The Lady

The People's Friend

The Railway Magazine

Saga Magazine

The Scots Magazine

This England

Animals/Nature Study

Cat World

Country Life

Country Walking

The Countryman

Dogs Monthly

Evergreen

Focus

Girl Talk

Home & Country

The Lady

This England

'How-to' and 'Things to do' Features

Amateur Gardening

Amateur Photographer

Cat World

Chat

Choice

Dogs Monthly

Essentials

Family Circle

Girl Talk

Homes & Gardens

Ideal Home

Junior

More!

Mother & Baby

My Weekly

The New Writer

19

Nursery World

Practical Family History

Practical Householder

Practical Parenting

Prima

Writers' Forum

Writers' News

Writing Magazine

Family Matters – Advice on Relationships, Children, etc.

Bella

Choice

Christian Herald

Eve

Family Circle

Junior

Mother & Baby

19

Nursery World

Practical Parenting

Red

She

Woman Alive

Woman & Home

'The Dating-and-Mating Game'

More!	She
19	

Personality Profiles/Interviews

Active Life	The New Writer
Best of British	19
Cat World	Red
Choice	Saga Magazine
Christian Herald	She
Crimewave	The Third Alternative
Eve	The Weekly News
Focus	Woman Alive
Good Housekeeping	Woman & Home
Homes & Gardens	Woman's Weekly
Interzone	Writers' Forum
Ireland's Own	Writers' News
My Weekly	Writing Magazine

Business/Financial Matters

Choice	Ideal Home
Essentials	Making Money
Homes and Gardens	Woman & Home

Travel

Active Life	The Lady
Choice	Prima
Home & Country	Woman's Weekly

The Magazine Writer's Handbook

Real Life/Personal Experiences

Active Life

Bella

Best

Cat World

Chat

Choice

Christian Herald

Family Circle

Good Housekeeping

The Lady

More!

Mother & Baby

My Weekly

Nursery World

Practical Parenting

Prima

Saga Magazine

That's life!

Wanderlust

The Weekly News

Woman Alive

Woman's Weekly

Writers' Forum

Writers' News

Yours

Articles for Young Children

Brownie

Collect it!

Kids Alive!

FICTION

Short-Short Stories – for Children

Brownie
Girl Talk
Ireland's Own
Kids Alive!
The People's Friend

Picture-Story Scripts – for Children

Girl Talk
Kids Alive!

Short Stories (1,000-plus words)

Active Life
Bella
Candis
Crimewave
Interzone
Ireland's Own
The Lady
My Weekly
The People's Friend
Prospect

The Scots Magazine
Take a Break's Fiction Feast
The Third Alternative
Woman & Home
Woman's Weekly
Woman's Weekly Fiction Special
Writers' Forum
Yours
And the 'Independent' magazines
(see Chapter 4 – page 105)

Short-Short Stories (single-page, up to about 1,000 words max)

Active Life

Bella

Best

Dogs Monthly

Ireland's Own

More!

My Weekly

Take a Break

Take a Break's Fiction Feast

That's life!

Woman

Woman & Home

Woman's Weekly

Woman's Weekly Fiction Special

Yours

Serials

My Weekly

The People's Friend

Woman & Home

Woman's Weekly

Poetry

Best of British

The Countryman

Evergreen

The People's Friend

The Scots Magazine

This England

See also the 'Independent' magazines
(Chapter 4 – page 105)

Letters and Fillers

Active Life

Amateur Gardening

Amateur Photographer

Antiques & Collectables

Autocar

Bella

Best

Best of British*

Brownie†

Candis

Interzone*

Ireland's Own*

Kids Alive!*

More!

Mother & Baby

My Weekly

19

Nursery World*

The People's Friend

Practical Householder

Cat World

Chat

Choice

Christian Herald*

Collect it!

Country Life*

Country Quest*

Country Walking*

Dogs Monthly*

Essentials

Essentially America*

Eve

Evergreen

Family Circle

The Field*

Focus*

Geographical

Girl Talk†

Good Housekeeping

Home & Country

Ideal Home

Practical Parenting*

Prima

Prospect*

The Railway Magazine

Reader's Digest

Red

Saga Magazine

The Scots Magazine*

She

Take a Break

That's Life!

This England

Wanderlust

The Weekly News

Woman

Woman & Home*

Woman's Own

Woman's Weekly

Writers' Forum*

Writers' News

Writing Magazine

Yours

* *No prizes or payment*
† *From children only*

4

ALTERNATIVE/ INDEPENDENT MAGAZINES

Many of the magazines reported on in Chapter 1 use short stories. But most of them are women's magazines and many of the stories have at least some romantic flavour. And some men are – quite unnecessarily – hesitant about offering their stories to women's magazines. As long as their stories match the requirements of the specific market, they'll have as good a chance as anyone of acceptance. (In this edition, I have excluded any magazine that discriminates against either sex.) Some of the women's magazines do use other-than-romantic short stories – ghost tales, twist-in-the-tail stories, (gentle) horror stories, etc., but these are often restricted to the short-short, 'coffee-break' story spot.

There are now only a few 'mainstream' magazines (among them, notably, *Crimewave* (page 36) and the SF specialist *Interzone* (page 50)) buying longer, 'literary', 'straight' or supposedly 'male-interest' short stories.

There are, however, many smaller magazines that welcome other-than-romantic short stories. Because they are out of the mainstream of commercial publishing though, many of these smaller magazines pay much less than the women's magazines. Some pay nothing at all. Some of the smaller magazines also welcome poetry – and one or two even pay for it. But they offer a chance to get your work published.

As I wrote in *Writers' Forum* (January 2001), 'Who else will welcome our quirky, off-the-wall short stories, our experimental poetry? ... Independent magazines don't have to please a corporate boardroom, profit-seeking shareholders or big-money advertisers. They can publish what they like – and what they like is innovative, cutting-edge prose and poetry which has no place in the high-powered commercialism of the world's IPCs and EMAPs.'

The downside of this independence is, of course, funding. A few magazines receive Arts Council grants, some manage to get sold from bookshops, but most survive entirely on subscriptions. They are nearly always produced on a minimal budget by a single enthusiast or a small team working in their spare time and relying on reciprocal advertising for publicity. Most of them struggle to keep subscription lists up to viable levels. Every editor I've spoken to gives the same advice: 'Please buy and read at least one copy of the magazine you want to write for. There is never a shortage of writers wanting to contribute material. Competition is tough, outlets limited, so you need to know what the editor likes.' So, subscribe if you possibly can, but at least buy a couple of back issues. (It's important, too, to look at your target magazines to make sure you'll be happy about the company your work would be keeping – you want to be proud of where you get published.)

The figures speak for themselves. It's well known in the business of Small Press poetry magazines that if every writer who submits material bought even a single copy of their target magazine, poetry would be bigger than any other part of the publishing business. Shelagh Nugent's *Reach Poetry* magazine, for example, receives 5,000 submissions a year and publishes about 600; Shelagh's prose magazine, *Peninsular*, publishes 40 out of 400-plus short stories submitted. This is the norm for independent magazines – submissions invariably exceed capacity. Given a stronger subscription base, independent magazines could expand and give a platform to far more aspiring writers. And Shelagh urges: 'Don't underestimate the clout of Small Press magazines. They're great showcases for talent, and can be a good jumping-off point to bigger and more lucrative markets – not necessarily better, but we all want to earn decent money, don't we? It's essential to study your market.'

Editors of independent magazines do the best they can to help writers get into print. Beth Rudkin of *Acorn* magazine takes a typical approach to the job: 'Production must be to the highest possible standard. Writers will not be encouraged unless the magazine they are published in looks good. That takes money, so it's a problem, but it should be every editor's aim. And it's important to remember that most writers put their all into their writing. If it has to be rejected, I feel I should do it gently, perhaps hinting at where it can be improved.'

The independent press is run by special people like these, who provide a valuable service for both writers and readers. It's a national treasure and it deserves our whole-hearted support.

The list (below) of independent magazines is extremely limited and incomplete. Some worthwhile magazines will inevitably have been missed out; some – hopefully few – of those listed will not survive.

Only the most successful independent magazines can offer more than a token payment, and many can give only complimentary copies.

The annual *Small Press Guide* from the publishers of this book (see page 2 for their address) has details of more than 350 independent UK magazines, giving you an excellent overview of possible outlets.

Looking further afield, a comprehensive listing of the world of small press magazines – entitled *Light's List* – is available from John Light, Photon Press, 37 The Meadows, Berwick-upon-Tweed, Northumberland TD15 1NY, price £2.50 post free (cheques and postal orders payable to John Light). *Light's List* is a 64-page A5 annual publication currently listing more than 1,450 small press magazines published around the world that welcome creative writing in English.

It is also worth subscribing to the bi-monthly magazine *The Fix* (see page 107) and the newsletter *Dragon's Breath* (see under 'Updating Market Information' page 157) – to keep up with the ever-changing world of independent magazines.

Mostly, the format of the magazine details listed below is self-explanatory, but a few points need clarification:

- Most of the small press magazines have very small circulations; the circulation groups used in Chapter 1 are therefore not applicable. All the small magazines have circulations in a Chapter 1 category (a). For compatibility therefore, category (a) is subdivided into:

a1 up to 100 copies per issue
a2 101 – 400 copies per issue
a3 401 – 800 copies per issue
a4 801 – 2,000 copies per issue
a5 over 2,000 copies per issue

- Magazines were invited to disclose the approximate number of stories, articles and poems they used each year ... and the approximate number of stories, articles and poems they are offered annually. This information – the freelance writer's *odds* – are listed as 'Chances'; thus, 20/200 means that from 200 offered manuscripts, 20 are used - acceptance chances of 1 in 10.

Almost every editor/publisher stresses the need for potential contributors to study their magazine before submitting material. Far too many would-be contributors submit *inappropriate* material: it's just a waste of time and postage. And, of course, if you want there to be a small press market for your work, the magazines must be kept alive - by subscribers. Buy them and read them – don't just write for them.

Acorn Magazine

(1998), Beth Rudkin, South Scarle, Newark, Notts NG23 7JW.

E-mail: Acornmag@aol.com

Price: £2.95 (subscription £16 per year).

Frequency: 6 issues a year.

Circulation: a3.

Size: A4, 40 pages.

Uses: Fiction, non-fiction, poetry.

Length: Fiction and non-fiction maximum 1,500 words; poetry maximum 40 lines.

Chances: Fiction 96/500, non-fiction 96/300, poetry 100/700.

Pays: Fiction £5 per 1,000 words; non-fiction £5 per piece; poetry £3 per poem; on publication; no free copies.

Response time: 3 weeks.

Advice: Originality in style and content is always welcome.

Acumen Literary Journal

(1985), Patricia Oxley, 6 The Mount, Higher Furzeham, Brixham, South Devon TQ5 8QY.

Price: £4.50 (subscription £12.50 per year).

Frequency: 3 per year.

Circulation: a4.

Size: A5, 130 pages.

Uses: Non-fiction, poetry. Welcomes articles about poetry and poetry-related subjects.

Length: Non-fiction maximum 3,000 words; poetry maximum 150 lines.

Chances: Non-fiction 30/50, poetry 150/100,000.

Pay: Non-fiction from £10 per 1,000 words, poetry £5 per poem; 1 free copy on publication.

Response time: Rejections decided in 1 week, decisions on the short-list take up to 14 weeks.

Advice: Ensure your name and address are on every sheet. Any publishable poem is short-listed. Poems for each issue are chosen from the short-list (150 poems on average). Please send books for review to Reviews Editor: Glyn Pursglove, 25 St. Albans Road, Brynmill, Swansea, Wales SA2 0BP.

Ambit

(1959), Martin Bax, Ambit, 17 Priory Gardens, London N6 5QY.

Price: £6 (subscription £24 per year).

Frequency: 4 per year.

Circulation: a5.

Size: 16in x 24in, 96 pages.

Uses: Fiction, poetry, art. Uses a dozen or so short stories per year. Appropriate artwork considered.

Length: Fiction up to 10,000 words. Poems – no specified length.

Chances: Fiction 12/1,600, poetry 300-400/2,400.

Pay: £5 per printed page; 2 free copies, then discount; on publication.

Response time: 4 to 16 weeks.

Advice: 'Try to look at a copy to avoid submitting inappropriate material.'

Buzzwords

(1999), Zoë King, Calvers Farm, Thelveton, Diss, Norfolk IP21 4NG.

E-mail: editor@buzzwordsmagazine.co.uk

Website: www.buzzwordsmagazine.co.uk

Price: £3 UK (subscription £18 UK, £20 RoW).

Frequency: 6 a year.

Circulation: a2.

Size: A5, 64 pages.

Uses: Fiction, poetry.

Length: Fiction 400 to 4,000 words; poetry 40 lines maximum.

Chances: Fiction 40/800; poetry 72/1,000.

Pay: NIL – 2 free copies.

Response time: About 12 weeks.

Advice: '*Please read a sample copy before submitting.* Our readership is international, and our requirements reflect this.'

Countryside Tales

(2000), David Howarth, Park Publications, 14 The Park, Stow on the Wold, Cheltenham, Gloucestershire GL54 1DX.

Tel: 01451 831053. E-mail: parkpub14@hotmail.com

Website: www.parkpublications.co.uk

Price: £3.00 (subscription £10.00 per year).

Frequency: 4 per year.

Circulation: a2.

Size: A5, 60 pages.

Uses: Fiction, non-fiction, poetry.

Length: Fiction 2,000 words maximum, non-fiction 1,000 words maximum, poetry 40 lines maximum.

Chances: Fiction 20/500, non-fiction 60/600, poetry 60/1,000.

Pay: £10 for best item in each category; one free copy to all contributors published, on publication.

Response time: 2 weeks.

Advice: We welcome all kinds of material with a countryside/rural theme. Short stories can be on any subject but should have a rural setting or theme. Poetry can be in any style with a countryside theme. Articles can be biographies, farming articles, wildlife/nature etc. We are particularly interested in memories of the countryside in past times – childhoods spent in the country etc. The editor is quite happy to discuss ideas on the phone. For contributors guidelines, send an s.a.e. to the postal address.

First Time

(1980), Josephine Austin, 'The Snoring Cat', 16 Marianne Park, Dudley Road, Hastings, East Sussex TN35 5PU.

Price: £3.50 + p&p (subscription £8 per year incl p&p).

Frequency: 2 per year.

Circulation: a4.

Size: A5, 80 pages

Uses: Poetry only.

Length: 30 lines maximum per poem.

Chances: Unspecified/2,000.

Pay: NIL – no free copies.

Response time: 8 weeks.

Advice: No s.a.e., no return of poems. Please write name and address on each poem.

The Fix - The Review of Short Fiction

(2001), Andy Cox, TTA Press, 5 Martins Lane, Witcham, Ely, Cambridgeshire CB6 2LB.

E-mail: ttapress@aol.com Website: www.ttapress.com

Price: £2.50 (subscription £15 for 6 issues).

Frequency: 6 issues per year.

Circulation: a5.

Size: B5 (240mm x 170mm), 40 pages.

Uses: Non-fiction only.

Length: Not specified.

Chances: Not specified.

Pay: Negotiable, plus one free copy, on publication.

Response time: 4 weeks.

Advice: Read The Fix! We review every magazine publishing short fiction in the English language, plus articles relevant to writers, market up-dates etc.

Good Stories

(1990), Andrew Jenns, 23 Mill Crescent, Kingsbury, Warwickshire B78 2LX.

Price: £4.00 (subscription £14.00 per year).

Frequency: 4 per year.

Circulation: a5.

Size: A5, 68 pages

Uses: Fiction only.

Length: Fiction 100 to 3,000 words.

Chances: Fiction 40/750.

Pay: Fiction £25 per 1,000 words, on publication. No free copies.

Response time: 16 weeks.

Oasis

(1969), Ian Robinson, 12 Stevenage Road, London SW6 6ES.

Price: £2.50 (subscription £6.00 for 4 issues - *not* per year).

Frequency: 3 per year.

Circulation: a2.

Size: A5, 32-36 pages.

Uses: Fiction, non-fiction, poetry.

Length: Fiction maximum 2,000 words; non-fiction maximum 2,000 words; poetry any length.

Chances: Fiction 3/10; non-fiction unspecified; poetry 5 to 10/350.

Pay: NIL; free copies on publication, number unspecified.

Response time: 2 weeks.

Advice: 'Study a few issues before submitting work.'

Obsessed With Pipework

(1997), Charles Johnson, 41 Buckley's Green, Alvechurch, Birmingham B48 7NG.

E-mail: flare.stack@virgin.net

Price: £3.50.

Frequency: 4 per year.

Circulation: a2.

Size: A5, 50 pages.

Uses: Poetry only.

Length: Any length.

Chances: 160/1,300.

Pay: NIL; one free copy on publication.

Response time: 6 to 8 weeks.

Advice: We tend to reject poems which are predictable and spell out a 'message'. If in doubt, delete more adjectives and even more adverbs.

Orbis

(1969), Carole Baldock, 17 Greenhow Avenue, West Kirby, Wirral CH48 5EL.

E-mail: carolebaldock@hotmail.com

Price: £4 (subscription £15 per year).

Frequency: 4 per year.

Circulation: a4.

Size: A5, 80 pages.

Uses: Fiction (see 'Advice' below), poetry, articles (commissioned only).

Length: Fiction minimum 500 words, maximum 1,000 words; poetry minimum 4 lines, no maximum specified but preferably not more than about 40 lines.

Chances: Not quantifiable – uses roughly 16 prose, 200 poems a year.

Pay: None as such, but one free copy to contributors and one Readers' vote prize (£50) plus Editor's Choice (£40, £30, £20, 3 x subscriptions) per issue, on publication. Response time: 6 to 8 weeks.

Advice: Basically a poetry magazine, *Orbis* also includes a few 'prose pieces' each year (i.e. more literary than formula/commercial fiction). Please study guidelines before submitting. And no s.a.e., no reply. You can sample *Orbis* at www.poettext.com

Peninsular

(1996), Shelagh Nugent, Linden Cottage, 45 Burton Road, Little Neston, Cheshire CH64 4AE.

Price: £3.50 (subscription £14.00 per year).

Frequency: 4 per year.

Circulation: a2.

Size: A5, 90-plus pages.

Uses: Fiction, non-fiction.

Length: Fiction 1,000 to 4,000 words; non-fiction 500 to 2,000 words.

Chances: Fiction 40/400; non-fiction 8/200.

Pay: £5 per 1,000 words; 1 free copy; on publication.

Response time: 2 weeks.

Advice: 'We consider work from both subscribers and non-subscribers *but* we do insist that potential contributors at least buy one current issue so they don't send us unsuitable material. There are guidelines and a submissions form in each issue. Read the guidelines, read the magazine, send a beautiful manuscript.'

Poetry Life

(1994), Adrian Bishop, No 1 Blue Ball Corner, Water Lane, Winchester, Hampshire SO23 0ER.

Website: http://freespace.virgin.net/poetry.life/

Price: £6.50 incl p&p (subscription £19.50 per year – plus £3.00 if outside the UK).

Frequency: 3 per year.

Circulation: a4.

Size: A4, 40 pages.

Uses: Poetry only.

Length: Not specified.

Chances: Figures not available.

Pay: 'To celebrate the publication of the 20th issue and to encourage the highest quality of writing Poetry Life Publishing will pay £250 for every *Poetry Life Recommendation* published in Poetry Life magazine from the 20th issue onwards. Five *Poetry Life Recommendations* per magazine will be published in each issue. One will be offered to the winner of the Poetry Life Open Competition and four will be offered to general submissions.'

Response time: 'Depends on amount of time available!'.

Information and advice: 'A *Poetry Life Recommendation* consists of a collection of about 5-6 poems from the poet. Previously published work is encouraged, as it is the intention that the collection represents the best of the individual poet's work. For consideration for a *Poetry Life Recommendation* please submit no more than seven poems at a time. Make sure your name and address and phone number are on all the poems together with an s.a.e.

'Fair's fair, as our only source of income is from magazine sales, we will only consider work from current subscribers to *Poetry Life* magazine. If there are insufficient magazine sales, Poetry Life reserves the right to reduce payments pro rata. The intention is that, not only is the best work of poets published, but Poetry Life has sufficient circulation to promote a national critical reputation for poets. Please make cheques payable to Poetry Life.'

Quantum Leap

(1997), Alan Carter, York House, 15 Argyll Terrace, Rothesay, Isle of Bute, Scotland PA20 0BD.

Price: £4.00 UK and EU, £4.50 Rest of Europe, £5.00/$10.00 US and Rest of World. (Subscriptions: £14.00 UK and EU, £16 Rest of Europe, £17.00/$34.00 US and Rest of World.)

Frequency: 4 per year.

Circulation: a2.

Size: A5, 40-plus pages.

Uses: Poetry only.

Length: Minimum 5 lines, maximum 40 lines..

Chances: 280/1,600.

Pay: £2.00 per poem, no free copies.

Response time: 2 weeks.

Advice: '*Quantum Leap* publishes poetry of all types, ranging from "classic" forms such as villanelles, sonnets and rondeaux, through experimental/concrete poetry, both serious and comic, and free verse. We publish poetry by its quality, not by name, so new writers have just as good a chance as established ones, but please send for our guidelines – s.a.e. or 2 IRCs to the above address – before submitting.'

Reach Poetry

(1996), Shelagh Nugent, Linden Cottage, 45 Burton Road, Little Neston, Cheshire CH64 4AE.

Price: £2.50 (subscription £30 per year).

Frequency: Monthly.

Circulation: a2.

Size: A5, 52 pages.

Uses: Non-fiction (reviews only), poetry.

Length: Poetry minimum 3 lines, maximum 80 lines.

Chances: Poetry 600/5000.

Pay: NIL; no free copies; £50 'Readers' Vote' prize each month.

Response time: 4 weeks.

Advice: 'We consider work from both subscribers and non-subscribers *but* we do insist that potential contributors at least buy one current issue so they don't send us unsuitable material. There are guidelines and a submissions form in each issue. Read the guidelines, read the magazine, send a beautiful manuscript.'

Scribble

(1999), David Howarth, Park Publications, 14 The Park, Stow on the Wold, Cheltenham, Gloucestershire GL54 1DX.

Tel: 01451 831053. E-mail: parkpub14@hotmail.com

Website: www.parkpublications.co.uk

Price: £3.00 (subscription £10.00 per year).

Frequency: 4 per year.

Circulation: a2.

Size: A5, 60-plus pages.

Uses: Fiction only.

Length: Maximum 3,000 words.

Chances: 60/1,000.

Pay: £50.00/£15.00/£10.00 for best 3 stories; one free copy to all contributors published, on publication.

Response time: 2 weeks.

Advice: 'Stories can be on any subject – humour, romance, horror, sci-fi etc. We are unlikely to publish stories containing excessive sex, violence or obscene language. Realistic dialogue is acceptable but the Editor reserves the right to cut offensive words. Although any subject will be considered, we do put the emphasis on entertainment. Therefore, stories with a beginning, middle and satisfactory conclusion are more likely to be accepted. As with any publication, it is strongly advised that potential contributors study at least one copy of the magazine before submitting material. Full guidelines can be obtained by sending an s.a.e. to the editorial address.'

Staple

(1982), Ann Atkinson and Elizabeth Barrett, Padley Rise, Nether Padley, Grindleford, Hope Valley, Derbyshire S32 2HE. Also 35 Carr Road, Walkley, Sheffield S6 2WY (subscriptions).

Price: £3.50 (subscription £10 per year - £15 non-UK).

Frequency: 3 per year.

Circulation: a3.

Size: A5, approximately 100 pages.

Uses: Fiction, non-fiction (articles), poetry.

Length: Fiction maximum 4,000 words; non-fiction maximum 3,000 words; poetry, no limits specified.

Chances: Fiction 20/700; non-fiction 6/20; poetry 120/7,000.

Pay: Fiction NIL; non-fiction £10; poetry £5 per poem. One free copy on publication – *or* 3 copies and no payment *or* 1 year's free subscription.

Response time: 6 to 8 weeks.

Advice: 'Read *Staple* before submitting, send 4 to 6 poems (min/max), always include an s.a.e., use an A5 or A4 envelope.

The Tabla Book of New Verse

(1992), Stephen James, Department of English, University of Bristol, 3-5 Woodland Road, Bristol BS8 1TB.

Price: £6.00 post free.

Frequency: Annually.

Circulation: a3.

Size: A5, 96 pages.

Uses: Poetry only.

Length: No restriction.

Chances: No information available.

Pay: On judging of annual competition; competition prize fund of £1,000 – see under 'Advice'.

Response time: Depends when work is submitted; usually within two months of competition closing date.

Advice: 'Each book contains selected competition entries, work by former contributors and poems by established authors. Poets new to *Tabla* are invited to approach via the competition in the first instance.'

Weyfarers

(1972), Martin Jones, Jeffery Wheatley, Stella Stocker, 1 Mountside, Guildford, Surrey GU2 4JD.

Price: £2.50 (subscription £6.00 per year).

Frequency: 3 per year.

Circulation: a2.

Size: A5, 36 pages.

Uses: Poetry and reviews.

Length: Poetry: minimum 4, maximum 50 lines.

Chances: 100/800.

Pay: NIL; 1 free copy.

Response time: 3 months.

Advice: 'Bright lively poems looked for. Any subject acceptable. Newcomers welcome.'

5

WRITING FOR MAGAZINES – THE BASIC PRINCIPLES

Make sure *before you send anything* that the market you have in mind is willing to consider freelance submissions

Look through the publication for a declaration of their policy on this (usually in small print in the masthead or at the back). You might find a statement on the lines of 'No responsibility taken for unsolicited mss', which indicates that such submissions will at least be looked at; or 'This publication does not accept any unsolicited material and cannot return it if sent', which means they won't even look at unsolicited material – so don't send anything without first querying the appropriate editor.

Reader profile

Draw up a profile of the person you see as the average reader of your target publication. (The advertisements will help here.) What age range? Social status? Financial status/spending power? Educational level? Interests? Try to have a picture of this average reader in mind as you think about the suitability of your short story or how you will treat your non-fiction topic.

Find a specific focus for your non-fiction article

Don't treat your topic in a general way, or try to include too many aspects in one piece. Find a particular angle from which to approach your subject, and focus on that. (Don't feel obliged to cram all the research you've done on your subject into one feature – you might have enough material for two or three pieces for different markets.)

Make sure that the content, style and language of your work are *suitable*

Content: It's essential to submit only material that is appropriate to your target publication. Your submission is certain to be rejected if your subject matter is alien to the publication's area of interest. *Hello!* won't be interested in a report on your local swimming gala – unless a celebrity is competing. *Amateur Photographer*'s readers don't expect to read about how to care for your cat.

Style: Does your target publication prefer a formal approach, with dense prose and longish paragraphs – or a more casual style with punchy paragraphs and possibly bullet points for emphasis? You'll reduce your chances if you don't write up your material in the publication's established style.

Language: Does the publication use words that are short and simple, or more sophisticated and multi-syllable? Are the sentences short and simply structured, or are they more complex, with subordinate clauses? Are the words, for the most part, colloquial or formal?

Get the length right

You can find the stipulated length requirements for many publications in the annual reference books. Many editors prefer to discuss length after they've assessed the value of your proposed feature, but you need to be aware of your target publication's length limitations so that you can suggest an appropriate wordage when you make your first approach. Editors have a certain amount of space to fill and they won't alter the size of their publication to accommodate an overlong feature, however interesting it might be. You'll do yourself a big favour (and avoid unnecessarily irritating the editor) by respecting the required length limits.

IMPORTANT: Make sure your market research is bang up to date – only look at current or very recent issues of your target publication for your market research – the whole market is so volatile these days that an issue produced even two or three months ago can give a misleading picture of current requirements.

The Most Saleable Article Types

Listed below are the types of magazine articles most in demand:

Interview - A person-to-person conversation, focused on the person being interviewed. Celebrity interviews are particularly popular.

Profile - A word-portrait of a person (or even an animal).

How-to - Showing readers how to do or make something, how to save time or money etc.

Self-help - A type of 'How To', but giving advice, guidance and encouragement in areas of human psychology and behaviour.

Personal experience - An article relating a first-hand experience, written in the first person (possibly as an '… as told to …' piece).

Inspirational - Sometimes called a **Brightener**. An article aiming to inspire hope and courage in its readers, often with a 'triumph over tragedy' slant.

Service - An article usually aimed at the consumer, giving a range of choices of product and possibly with advice on selection.

Round-up or **Survey** - A collection of comments, opinions, information, advice, quotes etc. on any topic, gathered from a number of experts, celebrities, people-in-the-street …

Essay, Commentary, Op-Ed (Op-Ed = Opinion-Editorial) - A personal opinion or a personal exploration of a subject or issue.

Historical - An article focusing on people, places and events in history.

Nostalgia - A fond look at the past, usually with a personal and positive focus, appealing to readers' sentiments and emotions. Usually has a strong 'those were the days …' flavour.

Anniversary - An article recalling, re-examining, or enlarging on a past event. Subjects can range from the famous to the local or the long-forgotten, and are featured in newspapers and magazines on or near the date of the event's anniversary.

Investigative/Exposé - An article reporting researched and documented information about an important, possibly controversial, subject.

General interest - A piece with broad reader appeal that doesn't fit into a specific category.

Humour - An article written specifically to amuse, as distinct from a 'straight' article written with a touch of humour. Often written in the first person.

6

SUBMISSIONS TO EDITORS — THE BASIC PRINCIPLES

There are always new writers starting up, needing to know how to submit their work to editors. Virtually every editor too, feels the need to remind writers that their work should be 'properly presented' – which suggests that it is not merely beginners who need this advice.

Even in these days of e-mail it will, in most cases, be sensible for at least your initial submission of work to a magazine to be in the form of 'hard copy' – typescript. Exceptions to this recommendation are when offering work to e-zines (electronic magazines) and – subject to the advice contained in any available guidelines – to overseas publications. So, for now, concentrate on typescript.

The presentation of your work – how it looks when it lands on the editor's desk – is of considerable importance; it separates the 'professionals' from the 'amateurs'; it is, in effect, the 'shop window' for your wares. Scruffy-looking work creates a bad first impression.

There are certain basic principles about the presentation of work, and also generally about approaching editors. These principles are:

- All work must be typescript, on white A4 paper, (297mm x 210mm) of about 80 gsm weight (not too thick, not too thin). If using continuous sheets of computer paper, remember to separate out the pages before submitting them. (Make sure they're all right-way-up too – and remove the hole-punched edges.)

- If you are (still) using a typewriter, it doesn't matter whether your work is typed in *pica* (10 characters per inch) or *elite* (12 per inch) typeface. Any 'ordinary' typewriter font will do. Just avoid 'fancy' typefaces, such as imitation joined-up writing or large and small capitals. And make sure that you have a fresh ribbon in your typewriter.

  But most people nowadays use a computer, with a word processor. Most WP (word processor) programs and printers offer you a wide choice of type-face/font. Restrict your choice to something fairly conventional and keep to a similar size to typescript. Very few 'mainstream' magazine editors want (or welcome) ready-to-print ('camera ready copy' = 'CRC') submissions.

  If you are (still) using a dot-matrix printer with your computer, consider changing to an ink-jet or laser printer. Neither of these is particularly expensive these days – and the output **looks** much better than 'dotty' typescript. Many editors, especially in the States, refuse to read dot-matrix-printed typescripts.

- The typescript page should be set-up to a standard format. Allow a 45-50mm (about two inches) margin on the left and at least 25mm (one inch) on the right. These wide margins are to provide room for the editor to make corrections and give instructions to the printers.

  (Most editors prefer word-processed typescripts NOT to be 'right-justified' – i.e., they like the right margin left uneven, as with a typewriter. This preference is because the process of right-justifying inserts extra gaps between words which may confuse the printer.)

- Begin a short story or article about one-third down the page with the title, in capitals, centrally on the line. Three or four single-spaced lines below this, type your own name or pen-name in lower case type, again – centred. Do not underline either title or byline. (Underlining means 'print in italics'.)

- Three or four more single-spaced lines beneath the title and byline, i.e., at about the centre of the page, begin the story or article proper. Don't indent the first paragraph but DO indent all subsequent paragraphs; maintain a common indent – usually of five spaces. (If writing an article, and providing sub-headings, don't indent the paragraph immediately beneath a sub-heading either.)

- Type the story or article *double-spaced*, that is, with a one-line space between lines of type. Do NOT leave an extra double-spaced line between paragraphs – as is customary in 'office' typing. (If providing sub-headings though, leave a blank, double-spaced, line above and below the sub-head; and it helps if you identify the sub-headings as such by a soft pencil annotation in the left margin.)

- Stop typing at least 25mm (one inch) – preferably more – from the foot of the page. Try to avoid carrying over a 'widow' – half a line at the end of a paragraph – onto the next page. (Carry over one-and-a-half lines rather than the half-line 'widow'.)

- At the top right corner of the second and all subsequent pages, provide a 'header' – something like 'Title/Wells/2'. The 'Title' in the identification should not be the full title but merely one or two key words from it. Leave about one double-spaced line between the header and the first line of the text proper.

- When you get to the end of your story or article, type a short, roughly central, row of dots followed by the word 'END'. Then, in the bottom left corner of the last page, type your (real) name and address, single spaced. (If using a pen-name, it is wise to indicate this by giving the name and address as 'Bill Bloggs, writing as Belinda Smith.') You may find it more convenient to provide the name and address in a single line, across the page, as I do. It matters not, as long as it's there.

- A cover page is a good idea for all articles and short stories. It should repeat the title in the centre of the page, with the *required* name centred below it. A few lines beneath the title and byline, record the word count. This should usually be to the nearest hundred words – never a precise figure. I mention the number of pages too, saying, 'Approximately 000 words on 0 sheets of typescript.' If it's an illustrated article, I add, 'accompanied by 00 photographs, by the author, and a caption sheet' (see below). Your name and address (as above if a pen-name) should again be typed at the bottom of the cover page.

- For stories, type 'FBSR (or 'First British Serial Rights') offered' in top or bottom right corner of the cover sheet. This identification of rights offered is seldom appropriate for articles: it will be assumed – and there are few markets for Second Rights of articles. (See below, for more on Rights.) Articles for the American market however, should always specify the rights offered. They often want First WORLD Rights.

- If you are submitting an illustrated article, you need to supply captions for the pictures. I usually provide these on a separate caption sheet which I append to the manuscript. Some editors and some writer-photographers favour the captions attached to the back of the photographs. It's your decision – or editorial preference.

  If you provide a separate caption sheet, ensure that each picture has an identification letter or number on the back to relate to the captions. Put a name sticker on the back of all illustrations too.

- I believe in sending a brief covering letter with every manuscript. (Many freelance writers do not.) The letter need only say, effectively, 'Here is an article/story about ... If you like it, please pay me at your usual rates; if you don't, please return it.' Letters look businesslike and if you have particular qualifications for writing a feature, are the place to tell the editor so, briefly.

- If the manuscript (story or article) is less than about 1,000 words in length and unillustrated, I fold it twice to fit into a DL-size (9' x 4 1/2') envelope. If longer, unillustrated, and not too bulky, I fold it in half. If illustrated, clearly the photographs should not be folded and must be protected with a sheet of cardboard. This, or a really bulky manuscript, may mean using a large, A4-size envelope. Always enclose an adequately-stamped self-addressed envelope *of the appropriate size* with every submission or query letter sent to an editor.

- Increasingly, editors are asking for a preliminary query rather than a complete submission of a feature article – even a short, under 1,000-word one. (This requirement is now indicated in the opening information paragraph on each market-report page in Chapter 1.) A query or article-outline needs to show the editor what the resultant feature will be about, its content, how you propose to treat it, and demonstrate that you understand the specific requirements of the magazine.

  A successful article-outline might take the form of a suggested title, the opening paragraph or two (the 'hook') and a list of the points that will be covered. The outline can also detail any special qualifications you may have for writing this particular feature.

  Many editors welcome – some insist on – photocopies of the writer's previously published work of a similar nature (and in a similar magazine) to that now proposed. (This, of course, makes it even more difficult for a beginning writer.)

Until you are known to an editor, you will seldom get a firm commission for a query-based feature article – but an expression of interest and a go-ahead are well on the way to an acceptance. It is important then to *quickly* deliver what you have offered – and make sure it is up to the outline's promise. When submitting, always remind the editor of his/her earlier interest.

Remember to enclose a stamped addressed envelope with every query. **Always** query longer articles – say 1,500 words-plus – even if editors don't insist on advance queries; it's to *your* advantage. And ... accept that not all editors will respond – at all – to queries, particularly if the suggestion doesn't interest them. (Even if you do provide an s.a.e.)

Queries are seldom appropriate for short stories – except where editors say that they don't want unsolicited fiction at all. (In which situation it would probably be wise to enclose a photocopy of an already published story of yours.)

• The most basic principle of all: write for a specific market. Don't write your story or article and then look for a suitable magazine to submit it to. The storyline needs of different magazines vary widely; different magazines want different approaches in their features too. The way to ensure that you hit the target is: first, read this *Handbook*; then, having selected a few specific magazines, study them in even greater detail. When you *really* know a magazine it is easier to produce suitable material for it. And – initially at least – concentrate on just a few magazines to 'attack'.

Footnote – on 'Rights'

When you offer a feature article to a British magazine the editor assumes that you are offering the first British publication of the article. (The 'FBSR' just confirms this.) The 'right', the copyright, is in *the way* in which the facts are presented, not the facts themselves. Once an article has been published – in any British publication, whether paid for or not, no matter how limited the circulation – you can never again offer FIRST British rights in that article. You *can* though, write another article on the same subject, using much the same set of facts, put together differently ... and offer FIRST British rights in that new piece. But DON'T offer similar articles simultaneously. There is virtually no market for second rights in articles; there is, for short stories.

The next six pages of the *Handbook* contain three ten-point checklists – one on writing style, and one each for the content of features and of short stories. Work through the relevant lists before despatch: they should help to improve the likelihood of your achieving publication.

(Note: similar versions of these checklists are also included in Gordon's book *Be A Successful Writer: 99 Surefire Checklists* [Allison & Busby].)

✔

10-Point Checklist ... on Writing Style

✔ Have you read your finished piece – article or short story – through, *aloud*? Reading aloud helps you identify the hard-to-read and/or pompous phrases that, from time to time, we all indulge in. It will also help you identify subject-object-verb inconsistencies.

✔ Are all your paragraphs roughly the same length? Make some of them shorter – the occasional single-sentence paragraph often lightens up your writing. Maybe join one or two 'same-subject' paragraphs together too – to achieve an overall variation.

✔ How long are your sentences? If too many of your sentences are over about 25 words, then your writing is probably not the desirable 'easy read'. An *average* sentence-length of about 15 words is a good target. But do vary the lengths within that average.

✔ Have you used too many 'difficult' words – ones whose meaning you had to check in the dictionary? (If you needed to check the meaning, so will your reader – who won't bother.) Remember: we're in the entertainment business; there's no captive market.

✔ Have you used many 'qualifying clauses' – such as added explanation, like this – in your writing? The sentence containing the explanatory clause is often better rewritten. Keep it simple.

✔ Have you 'murdered your darlings'? By that, in this instance, I mean those sentences and paragraphs of which you are particularly proud; the phrases you have written so well. Rewrite them – more simply. Don't try to impress the reader with the quality of your writing. Just 'communicate'.

✓ Does your writing still 'flow'? Shorter sentences and paragraphs, while easy to read, can lead to a rather 'bitty', jumpy style. Provide linking words and phrases between paragraphs. These links may only need to be an occasional 'and', 'also' or 'furthermore'.

✓ Do the first sentences in most paragraphs – particularly in articles – 'signal' the subject of the rest of the paragraph? The rest of each paragraph should expand on that initial thought. (And, of course, just one topic per paragraph. You can write several paragraphs on one topic but never two topics in one.)

✓ Have you qualified the unqualifiable? Too often, one reads phrases such as 'very unique' – which is rather like being 'slightly pregnant'. Avoid this … like the plague. And watch out for such clichés. If you must use a cliché, invent your own.

✓ Have you gone through your near-final draft and *pruned* it? Most drafts can be much improved by a ten per cent cut. The end result is inevitably 'tighter' – and usually more readable.

✓

10-Point Checklist ... Articles

✓ You DID write the article with a market in mind, didn't you? Different magazines have – maybe slight, but always significant – different requirements and styles. You must write for a specific market. So there's no question now, about where you're going to submit it, is there?

✓ Knowing the market, is the article the *right length*? It's no good submitting a 1,500-word article to a magazine that never uses anything longer than 800-word single-page articles. No, the editor will not cancel that advertisement to fit your article in.

✓ Is the article as a whole an *easy read* – or does the reader have to work at understanding what you're getting at? To ensure an *easy read*, keep your writing style simple and straightforward – short sentences, short paragraphs and no 'hard' words for which a reader might need to consult a dictionary. They won't.

✓ Have you a good title for your article? Keep it as punchy as possible; it's the first thing the editor (and hopefully, later, the reader) notices. And does it give some indication of what the article is about? (A punning title may not initially be clear, but it will become clear after the article has been read; this is fine.)

✓ Do you have a good 'hook' – a good opening paragraph? If you haven't seized the reader's attention in the first four or five lines, you're never going to get it.

✓ Does the end of the article round it all off neatly, tying up any loose ends – and perhaps reflecting the 'attention grabber' used in the hook?

✓ Does the content of the article conform to a realistic and understandable sequence; do the comments follow logically, one after the other ... or does it jump about like a flea on a mattress? Fleas are irritating.

✓ Does the content of the article live up to the promise of the title and, most important, stick to the point? There are few worse faults in an article than starting off on one subject and ending on a totally different one. Stick to one subject; use the other for another article.

✓ Have you gone back over your article and polished it – trimming off the waffle and the repetitions, shortening the over-long sentences, clarifying the meanings? Good articles are never just written – they're re-written.

✓ By the time he/she reaches the end of your article will the reader feel satisfied ... or merely sigh and say, 'So what?' Your article must entertain or – in an *acceptable* manner, because you can't force anyone to read it – instruct the reader. Would YOU want to read your article if it were by someone else?

✓

10-Point Checklist ... Short Stories

✓ Are the characters in your story compatible with the magazine's readership? It's no good offering a teenage magazine a story about granny – even one of today's swinging grannies – or vice versa. Your main characters should be around the same age as the target readership; readers like to be able to *identify* with them.

✓ Is your story the right length? More and more magazines are moving towards the short-short story – maximum length of about 1,000 words. (Individual magazines have their own specific length requirements: a hundred words over or under may make all the difference between rejection and acceptance. Check what they use, what they want.)

✓ How many characters appear in your short story? There is seldom room in a short story for more than a (small) handful of characters. If you need 'a cast of thousands' ... write a novel. And, a sub-question, are your characters *alive* – or made of cardboard?

✓ Have you started the story *late enough*? Short stories can often be improved by cutting out the first half dozen paragraphs. Start as near to the end of your story as possible – at, or immediately before the crisis that leads to the essential *change*.

✓ Following on: does the main character *change* – develop his/her personality, overcome some adversity, learn something perhaps, as a result of the action in the story? The change need not be anything world-shattering – but it must be there.

✓ Still on the same general point: is there a *conflict*? Conflict between characters, conflict with the elements, conflict with a conscience, conflict with 'the way things are'? The shorter stories may have only a single conflict; longer stories perhaps more than one. But without conflict, there is no story at all. And the conflict must be linked to the change.

✓ Have you described your main character sufficiently for the reader to picture – but without a full biography (for which there is insufficient room in a short story)?

✓ Have you included some/enough dialogue? A short story that is wholly introspection or description is usually hard to read. Dialogue makes a story come alive; it lightens up the read. (It also makes a story *look* easier to read.)

✓ Does your storyline plot spring naturally from the characters – or is it forced, with the characters made to act out their parts like cardboard cut-outs? Plot should come from character.

✓ Does your story start with a strong hook – and end with a *satisfying*, believable conclusion? Does the opening paragraph really grab you? And does the last paragraph leave a good taste in the mouth – without going into unnecessary details?

7
WRITING A COLUMN

As you will have seen from the reports in Chapter 1, most magazines use regular columns on various aspects of their core interests. These columns are often written either by staff or by regular contributors. Some of these writers might be experts in a specific field like medicine, child-care, the law and so on, and some might be there because their names are well-known to the public and enhance the magazine's popularity. Other columnists, though, are there because they have a track record in writing about a specific subject which that magazine's readers enjoy and value.

Perhaps you've already published a few articles on a subject that particularly interests you: a hobby or special interest, your career or life experiences. Maybe you've written about religion, spirituality, health and fitness, family relationships, home-making, bringing up children, leisure interests, sport, computers, finance, business, travel, cooking ... You'll have the greatest chance of success if you write on a topic you feel strongly about and in which you have an abiding interest. Writing a column takes stamina and on-going enthusiasm.

There might be an opening for a column in one of the magazines you've already written for. Check out your local newspaper, too – perhaps there's a gap in their coverage you might be able to fill on a regular basis. (Make sure you get a fair financial return for your work, though; if it's worth publishing it's worth reasonable payment.)

Editors are especially keen to find columnists who can write about controversial topics without causing offence. Controversy generates publicity and gets readers involved with the publication.

To break in, you need to know your market. As with any other kind of submission, it's a waste of everybody's time to offer an editor a column on a topic that's inappropriate to his or her publication.

You also need to demonstrate that there's no danger of you running out of steam – or ideas – after just a few columns. Prepare three or four complete columns, plus detailed outlines for three or four more, and one-line ideas for a further half-dozen.

If your proposed topic has associated products, try to ferret out some financial information to help sell your column to the editor. For example, if you write about computer games, research how much the companies who make them spend on advertising. This kind of information will help your target editor convince his or her company that your column could help sell advertising space.

Here are a few tips to help you get started:

- Know your audience. It's vital to understand the interests and concerns of the people you're writing for. Many magazines produce a media pack that includes readership profiles and demographics. (Some of them publish such information on their websites.) Use this information to supplement your own market research and analysis.

- Know your topic inside out and from every angle. You don't need a degree to write about, for example, collecting ceramics, but you do need to know the factories, designers, identification marks, dates, auction houses, experts, restoration techniques and so on.

- Focus each column on a narrow area within your subject niche. Readers want details and specific information, not generalities.

- Keep meticulous records of sources and transcripts of interviews – you might be called on to produce them.

- Write fairly and accurately. Don't invent 'experts' or sources of quotations.

- Write with authority. You know your topic thoroughly – make sure you convey your knowledge with confidence.

- Encourage your readers to write to you. Answer the letters, and make sure your editor knows about them. A columnist who generates a substantial reader-correspondence is of on-going value to the publication.

- Meet deadlines. It's a good idea to provide the editor with a few back-up columns on aspects of your topic that won't date, to be held on file in case of illness or any other unforeseeable event that prevents you delivering your column on time.

- Think ahead for seasonal aspects of your topic.

- Accept with good grace any changes the editor makes to your column. *A little bit of advice*: If you want to challenge any change you don't agree with, have a very good reason for doing so, and plenty of ammunition to back up your argument. Remember, it will be easier for the editor to find another columnist than for you to find another regular slot.

8

WRITING PICTURE-STORY SCRIPTS

Picture-story scripts offer an outlet for the fiction writer that is often overlooked. D. C. Thomson (particularly) publish a number of weekly magazines filled with drawn or photographed picture-stories; and welcome scripts from freelance writers. And there are other magazines which use the occasional picture-story. D. C. Thomson publish such magazines as *The Beano* and *The Dandy*, as well as the longer, book-length picture stories such as *Commando*. Each picture-magazine uses several picture-stories each week, and there are at least two book-length stories in each series, each month. (Two a week from *Commando*!) There are plenty of opportunities. In their usual helpful way, D. C. Thomson will provide interested writers with a whole sheaf of advice on their requirements, and how best to meet them. (Write – with a large stamped addressed envelope of course – to Fiction Department [Picture-scripts], D. C. Thomson & Co Ltd, Courier Place, Dundee DD1 9QJ.)

Picture-stories are much like any other form of fiction: they entail the use of the customary story-telling skills, plus a few extra techniques. There is virtually no difference in the writer's approach to drawn or photo-illustrated picture-stories: the scenery can be more exotic in a drawn story; photo-stories use everyday backgrounds. The writer starting in this field should, of course, study the market before having a go; it may also help to outline some of the more basic 'rules':

- The writer is not required to provide the illustrations (drawn or photographic) for the story and should not attempt to do so. All that is required from the writer is a script. Picture-stories are told in a specific number of pictures, known as 'frames' or 'panels'; for each frame, the writer must provide all the details.

- Like any other work of fiction, the obvious and basic need is a good story. This needs – even more than usual – to have: a gripping opening, to grab the reader's interest; a strong, uncomplicated plot, complete with atmosphere and a small cast of really believable characters; and a good, powerful ending to the tale, tying up all the loose ends.

- For each frame in the story, the writer must provide:

  ✓ a brief description of the scene portrayed, from which the artist/ photographer will work (and see below for more on viewpoint);

  ✓ the characters' necessary dialogue and thoughts (a particularly useful technique this) to be displayed in speech or thought 'balloons'; and

  ✓ any necessary caption (see below).

- Speech, thoughts and captions alike should all be kept as brief as possible. There is no scope in a picture-story for a lengthy soliloquy; all speech and thoughts must carry the action forward. Descriptive material should usually be *shown* in the picture and therefore left unsaid. It is a good idea to aim at a *total* length of speeches, thoughts and captions in any one frame of about 25 words – and preferably less. Basically, the shorter the better.

- The personalities of the characters in the picture-story should be brought out through the dialogue, the thoughts and the action – not by lengthy descriptions. The captions should be restricted to no more than is necessary to perhaps replace a series of static action-less pictures, or simply to establish the time, for instance 'Next morning'.

- The description of the scene portrayed in each frame should be as brief as possible. It is best to allow the artist/photographer to use his/her own imagination as much as possible in setting the scene. The photographer will fit the story to whatever is suitable and readily available. (You can have whatever you like, if it is to be drawn – but non-essential detail is up to the artist.) The writer need only say, for instance, 'Close-up: Val is slumped on her bed, weeping.' It is seldom necessary to describe the bedroom and its furniture; Val herself will already have been described.

- When thinking about and then describing the pictures to be drawn or photographed, not only must you 'think visual', you must also try to introduce variety. You can vary both the scene and the viewpoint. (To a conventional fiction writer 'viewpoint' means the character through whose eyes and thoughts the story is seen and told; to a picture-story writer the viewpoint is the position from which the picture is viewed – like a camera position.) If your hero is in difficulties – or thinking – the picture must concentrate on him; the viewpoint you choose will not be that of the hero but that of the artist/photographer.

  The viewpoint can also vary by, for instance, zooming in from a wide-screen identification shot to an extreme close-up of an anxious face. When two characters are in conversation, the sequence of frames might alternate from a viewpoint behind one (looking at the face of the other) to the opposite view. You can select a bird's eye view or a worm's eye view; you can watch your characters approach the viewpoint – or watch them walk away.

  At all costs, avoid a series of frames all with a similar view, with just talk and little or no action. Vary the viewpoint.

- Restrict the number of characters and locations used: remember that each person photographed has to be paid for and that each person has to be transported to each fresh location; if drawn, the more characters and locations, the more imagination the artist has to employ – and the more potentially confusing the resultant story. Ensure too, in your script, that the characters are significantly different in appearance and that their names are not confusingly alike.

- Picture-story scripts should be typed on the customary A4 paper, in double-spacing. Allow an extra wide left margin; in that, type the frame number and alongside, provide the description; beneath that, type the speeches and thoughts, using the left margin again to identify the person speaking or thinking; and when necessary, type 'Caption' in the margin and the words alongside. Usually, restrict each page of A4 to just two frames.

- You can ask for more exotic settings for drawn picture-stories than you can for photo-stories. Period costumes, sun-kissed desert-island settings or crowd scenes cost no more, when drawn, than two present-day teenagers cuddling on a settee.

- Most picture-story scripts are purchased outright. You will almost certainly be required to sell 'All rights' rather than the more usual 'First British Serial Rights'. Once sold, you will receive no further payments, no matter how often the publisher re-uses the story – in other languages, for instance.

The Magazine Writer's Handbook

For further advice, Dave Taylor (who writes scripts for, among others, D. C. Thomson) has written an excellent book on writing picture-story scripts, *A Guide to Comicscripting* (Robert Hale), 1993. The book is itself in picture-story form throughout.

Another excellent how-to book is *How to Draw and Sell ... Comic Strips* (Titan Books) 1998. Although this is aimed primarily at artists, the author, Alan McKenzie, is an experienced picture-script writer and editor and the book offers much useful advice for script-writers too. It also has a lot of useful information on picture-script *thinking*.

9

WRITING 'LETTERS TO THE EDITOR'

The beginning writer needs to get into print as quickly as possible – if for no other reason, to give his/her *ego* a boost. Writing 'Letters to the Editor' is one good way to achieve this. No, not writing to *The Times* to say that you've seen the first (or the last) cuckoo, nor writing to your local newspaper complaining about the rubbish in the streets. Rather, write to the editors of those magazines that *pay* for letters. If an editor pays for your letter, you will have sold your first piece of writing.

Many experienced freelances continue regularly to write letters to magazines' 'Letters' pages; it becomes a permanent part of their writing 'business'.

The payment for letters is not insignificant: few magazines pay less than £5 for a letter which need only be a hundred words long. That is £50 per thousand words. There is often also the possibility of a much bigger payment or a valuable prize for a 'star' letter. (In any case, one sold letter per week will go a good way towards paying for a holiday.) And you don't even need any equipment to write saleable letters – not even a typewriter.

Ground rules for writing 'paid-for' letters are:

- The letters should be short and to the point. Forty or fifty words may be enough to gain publication; 200 words will often be over-long. Within those length constraints, get to the point quickly and as soon as it's made, sign off. Make sure though, that the point is clear. (It's all good training for other forms of writing.)

- Be provocative, informative, or amusing; preferably all three at the same time. Editors like letters that stir other readers to respond to them, and if you can make an editor chuckle, you're made.

- Be personal, and original. Forget all the usual advice about avoiding the personal pronoun. Use it frequently: 'I think ...', 'I told ...', 'I went ...'. Write about your own experiences; don't offer second-hand ideas (unless writing about what 'my old gran used to tell me ...').

- Be topical. Don't, for instance, write about Christmas in mid-summer. (Allow for editorial lead times though, just as you would for an article: submit date-related letters at least three months early for a monthly magazine and six weeks ahead for a weekly.)

- Target your letters carefully. Although a general-interest magazine might accept and publish an unusual recipe or DIY hint, a specialist magazine may be more likely to take it, possibly for a bigger payment. But sometimes the reverse applies; so think before you despatch.

- Don't send a letter on the same subject to more than one magazine at a time. Many editors insist that letters be original (of course) and not previously published. (But that doesn't mean you can't, at some later date, write up the same episode/story in a different way: just don't send them out at the same time – a twelve-month gap will seldom hurt a good story.)

- Wait at least three or four months before you assume a letter is not to be used; you can then try it, or a similar letter, on another 'letters' column.

- Don't try to look like a professional writer. That is not at all what the editor wants, in this context. By all means type your letter if you have a typewriter (and if you're going to be a writer, you must have), but don't use a business letter-heading, and certainly don't double-space. (Do though, leave nice wide margins for editorial alterations.) And if you don't type your letter, do write legibly.

- Don't send a stamped self-addressed envelope or return postage (unless you are enclosing a potential 'happy snap'); don't ask for a free copy of the issue in which your letter is used; don't tell the editor how to pay you. Make your letter look as though it comes from an 'ordinary reader'. That is who the editor wants to hear from; some editors do not welcome letters from 'professional letter writers'. (One editor even keeps a black-list of those who write 'too regularly'.)

- Finally – study the market carefully, just as you would for a feature article or short story. Different editors, different magazines, require different types of letter.

Some magazines also welcome other 'fillers' - brief hints, tips, jokes, etc, sometimes on the 'letters' page, sometimes filling an end-of-page gap elsewhere. These too are good, albeit often small, money-spinners. You can, *if you wish* (but it's not essential), be more professional in submitting fillers: double-spaced typing, several at a time, but no more than one item per half-A4 sheet. Don't forget to put your name and address on each sheet, but don't bother with a stamped addressed envelope - you won't get them back.

If you use a pen-name for some of your letters, it is possible that you could experience problems in cashing payment-cheques made out in that name. Depending on the amounts involved, it might – but I doubt it – just possibly be worth the considerable hassle of opening a second bank account: 'Gordon Wells, trading as Judy Bloggs'. A possibly easier solution is to write your letters using the names of mother, sisters, daughters, etc. – as long as you can get the money out of them.

For much more advice on all aspects of letter- and filler-writing, see Alison Chisholm's *How to Write Five-Minute Features*, one of the Allison & Busby Writers' Guides. It's great: I heartily recommend it.

10
GETTING TOGETHER

Writing is a lonely occupation; you alone can commune with that blank sheet of paper, or the empty screen with the cursor blinking urgently at you. Most of us find we benefit from time spent in the company of other writers. Many people, when starting to write, are unaware of the opportunities for getting together with others at a similar stage in their writing development, or with those who have 'been there, learnt that', and progressed. And most writers are happy to pass on the benefits of their experience – to 'put back' some of what they themselves have gained.

Writers can get together at writers' circles (there are such groups of enthusiasts throughout the country), and at various writers' schools and conferences. It's also worth subscribing to one of the writing magazines.

Writers' circles

There are hundreds of writers' circles thriving all over the country. It is well worth investigating one near you. There are several ways of finding your nearest circle: ask at your library, they will probably know of the local club; look in your local newspaper, they often list their activities; or buy a copy of Jill Dick's excellent *Directory of Writers' Circles*, which lists just about every writers' circle in the country, including postal circles, which operate for the benefit of those who can't conveniently attend a group in person.

This directory is compiled and regularly up-dated by author/journalist Jill Dick. It is available from her at 'Oldacre', Horderns Park Road, Chapel-en-le-Frith, High Peak SK23 9SY. The price is £5.00 post free.

A warning: a writers' circle is only as useful as the writing ability, experience – and enthusiasm – of its members; beware the mutual admiration of non-achievers more interested in local gossip than the hard work of 'real' writing. If your aim is to achieve publication – and if not, why bother? – ask about the published works of other circle members.

Evening classes

All over Britain, Local Education Authorities or WEA committees organise evening classes in writing. Once again, the best first contact is your local library. The quality and value of the evening classes will also depend on the achievements and/or teaching ability of the tutor; most are dedicated to the task of developing and encouraging new writing talent. (There are some excellent tutors who have achieved little publication themselves – but are expert at bringing out talent in others.) It is worth investigating these opportunities in your area.

But beware courses not aimed at getting work published. Some courses are clearly and specifically intended for literary study; others aim at therapy. (If you want to become a *published* writer, go for a course entitled 'Writing for Pleasure and Profit' or similar, rather than one offering just 'Creative Writing'; the word 'profit' in the title suggests a more focused attitude.)

The Writers' Summer School – Swanwick

The five-day annual Writers' Summer School, held each August at The Hayes Conference Centre, Swanwick, Derbyshire, is the oldest-established – and by far the best – of the British writers' conferences. The first 'Swanwick', as it is known by all writers, was held in 1949 and it has been held in the same place every year since.

Swanwick offers five full days of concentrated advice on all aspects of writing for publication. Most days there are two formal lectures – one at 9.30 in the morning, the other after dinner. These lectures are by leading figures in the writing and publishing world; the list of past speakers resembles a Who's Who of Writers.

As well as the main talks there is a choice of half-a-dozen or more courses – each of five lectures – running concurrently throughout the week. The subjects vary from year to year but there is always something for everyone: beginners and well-established writers alike, of both fiction and non-fiction. Some courses include 'homework' during the week – but this is never too demanding.

The Magazine Writer's Handbook

As well as the courses there are dozens of less formal talks, two-lecture mini-courses and discussion groups filling the days; there is seldom an empty moment, and usually a choice of half-a-dozen such activities at any time. The last (optional) talk/discussion may not finish until nearly 11 pm – and after that there is (even more optional) dancing until 1 am every night except Sunday.

To get to Swanwick, send a business-sized (DL size) stamped self-addressed envelope to The Secretary, Jean Sutton, 10 Stag Road, Lake, Sandown, Isle of Wight PO36 8PE. Tel: 01983 406759. Application forms are sent out in late January; in the past, there was great competition for a place at Swanwick and application forms had to be returned immediately. Nowadays, the odd place is usually still available until somewhat nearer the School date.

The cost is increasing each year with inflation. Expect to pay about £200 for the standard accommodation (usually in single rooms without *en suite* bathrooms) £300-plus for more luxurious accommodation. The fee covers full board and accommodation from Saturday tea-time to Friday morning, plus all lectures and courses. Initially, you will get an acceptance receipt – or your money back; the programme, etc. arrives in July.

It is always a stimulating week.

The Writers' Holiday - Caerleon

There is another week-long writers' 'get-together': it lacks the long history of Swanwick but is increasingly popular. This is the Writers' Holiday organised at Caerleon – in Wales – by Anne Hobbs in late July each year.

A Caerleon Sunday-to-Friday 'holiday' is somewhat more relaxed than a Swanwick 'school' – nevertheless, much valuable tuition is packed in. 'Holiday-makers' can attend their choice of two (usually from ten or twelve) five-session morning courses. There are also many workshop sessions, usually in the afternoons. There are 'one-off' afternoon and evening talks; there is a choice of free excursions to local attractions one afternoon and an 'entertainment' (usually a Welsh choir) on the last evening.

Accommodation at Caerleon is in single student-type bedrooms with *en suite* bathrooms; every effort is made to separate (noisy) early-risers from (noisy) late-to-bedders – in separate residential blocks. Food is good.

To get on a Caerleon Writers' Holiday, write to D. L. Anne Hobbs, School Bungalow, Church Road, Pontnewydd, Cwmbran, South Wales NP44 1AT at any time with a stamped addressed envelope for details and a booking form. (Reservations are accepted up to a year ahead against a small non-returnable deposit.) Total cost about £330. (You can try phoning Anne Hobbs, on 01633-489438.)

Other writers' conferences

As well as the longer conferences at Swanwick and Caerleon, there are a number of week-long courses, annual weekends, and one-day writers' get-togethers around the country. These conferences, particularly the shorter events, are popular with writers and places are often at a premium. To be sure of a place, send a stamped addressed envelope for an application form about six months before the conference date; then, when you get the application form, reply swiftly.

The Arvon Foundation runs residential courses throughout the year at four centres around the UK, covering every kind of writing from poetry to novel-writing and journalism. Each course lasts for four-and-a-half days. The Arvon Centres are at Totleigh Barton at Sheepwash, Devon, Lumb Bank at Heptonstall in West Yorkshire, Moniack Mhor at Beauly in Inverness-shire and The Hurst near Ludlow in Shropshire. Grants are available for those who cannot afford the full fees. A brochure detailing all the courses, terms and so on can be obtained from the National Administration office, address: The Arvon Foundation, 2nd Floor, 42A Buckingham Palace Road, London SW1W 0RE. Tel: 020 7931 7611. Fax: 020 7963 0961. You can find out more about the Arvon Foundation and see details of all the courses at the website: www.arvonfoundation.org

The more important weekends for writers are, in date order:

- South Eastern Writers (SEWA) Conference: a weekend in March/April, in a comfortable country motel at Bulphan, Essex (near the M25). Main speakers and specialist lectures. Cost: about £160. Contact: Secretary – SEWA, *via* Marion Hough, 47 Sunningdale Avenue, Leigh-on-Sea, Essex SS9 1JY.

- South and Mid-Wales Association of Writers' (SAMWAW) Weekend: in mid-May, at Abergavenny, near Cardiff. Main speakers and specialist lectures. Cost: about £100. Also two annual one-day events, in February and October, costing about £25 each. Contact: Julian Rosser, SAMWAW, c/o IMC Consulting Group, Denham House, Lambourn Crescent, Cardiff CF4 5ZW. Tel: 029 2076 1170. E-mail: imc@i-dial.net

- Southern Writers' Conference: a mid-June weekend at the attractive Earnley Concourse near Chichester in West Sussex. Excellent food, excellent accommodation (mostly shared twin-bedded rooms), five main speakers and three three-stream talk/discussion group sessions. Cost: about £165. Application forms available in January from: Lucia White, Stable House, Home Farm, Coldharbour Lane, Dorking, Surrey RH4 3JG. Tel: 01306 876202.

- Winchester Annual Writers' Conference: a late-June weekend in a further education college in Winchester – with student-type accommodation. A number of workshops/courses on Friday evening and Sunday morning; Saturday is the main day, with 60 multi-stream talks (12 simultaneous one-hour streams, five sessions in the day.) and one-to-one advice interviews throughout the day. Cost: about £50 for the Saturday alone (excluding lunch), or about £165 for the full-board weekend. Further workshops during the week after – at extra cost. Details, programme, etc., from: Barbara Large, MBE, 'Chinook', Southdown Road, Shawford, Winchester, Hants SO21 2BY. Tel: 01962 712307. E-mail: WriterConf@aol.com

- The National Association of Writers' Groups (*see page 162*) has a weekend Festival of Writing in September, at St Aidan's College, Durham.

One-day writers' events – usually on a Saturday – abound. There are lots of one-day writing courses organised by local education authorities, at around £15–£20 for tuition only; but perhaps more interesting to the already-practising writer are the 'Days' and seminars organised by various local writing circles. Watch for announcements in the writing magazines for details. Most cost about £40 (including lunch) and are excellent value for money. Particularly good – and well-established – annual 'days', are:

- Southport Writers' Seminar: first Saturday in October, in Southport. (The 1999 Seminar was their 25th.) Contact: Jessie Mayberry, 30 Kingswood Drive, Crosby, Liverpool L23 3DE. (Tel: 0151 236 3397.)

- West Sussex Writers Club 'Day for Writers': October, at Durrington, on the outskirts of Worthing. Contact: Day for Writers Organiser *via* Nina Tucknott, 103 Poplar Avenue, Hove, East Sussex BN3 8PJ. (Tel: 01273 882625.)

(See also the SAMWAW one-day events, and the 'main' Saturday of the Winchester Conference, above, within the weekend details.)

NOTE: The contact names for each of the conferences, weekends and days can change from year to year. It is therefore helpful to include the title of the event alongside the person's name on the envelope (particularly those marked '*via*', and maybe mark the envelope 'Please Forward'); where appropriate, this enables retired organisers to forward the correspondence unopened (and without incurring extra postage costs) to their successors. It's in your own best interest.

11
COMPETITIONS

No ordinary spare-time writer – particularly of short stories or poetry – can afford to ignore competitions. They are often the only way – apart from self-publication – that even slightly adventurous poets or 'un-romantic' short story writers can get their work noticed. And the rewards from some of the competitions can be substantial.

The prizes may not be in the same league as the Booker, Trask, Whitbread, or Orange awards for novelists, but several offer quite significant amounts of money. And any prize - particularly those that also publicise the writer's name – can be invaluable to a short story writer or poet. It could lead to paid publication elsewhere.

The most important advice we can give to any writer considering entering a short story or poetry competition is ...

READ – AND COMPLY STRICTLY WITH – THE RULES

... and, when sending for details, rules, closing date, fees, etc., ALWAYS enclose a stamped addressed envelope.

Short Story Competitions

Listed below are some of the well-established and continuing short story competitions. There are many others, including some that are held only once – for a special occasion perhaps. The short story writer must always be on the watch for announcements of competitions in newspapers and magazines. Each of the writing magazines (see Chapter 1) publishes details of *some* competitions, including, of course, their own.

The two writers' market newsletters/magazines – *Freelance Market News* and *Writers' Bulletin* (see Chapter 12, page 157) – are the best sources for details of forthcoming competitions; they include many more than do the mainstream magazines. (*Freelance Market News* also runs its own occasional short story and poetry competitions.)

The useful bi-monthly publication *Competitions Bulletin* is dedicated to writing competitions. It's edited by Carole Baldock and published, like *Writers' Bulletin*, by Cherrybite Publications. Subscribe to any number for £2 each, post free. Cheques, payable to Cherrybite Publications, should be sent to them at Linden Cottage, 45 Burton Road, Little Neston, Cheshire CH64 4AE.

Some well-established competitions are:

- The Bridport Prize: annually (since 1980). Closing date 30th June. First prize £3,000. (See also their poetry competition – below.)

  Details: Competition Secretary, The Bridport Prize, Bridport Arts Centre, South Street, Bridport, Dorset DT6 3NR.

  Website: www.bridportprize.org.uk

- The Jo Cowell Award: Annually (since 1989). First prize £200 plus Jo Cowell Shield. Run by Ormskirk Writers and Literary Society.

  Details: Competition Coordinator, OWLS, Stone Cross, 2 Cobbs Brow, Newburgh, Wigan WN8 7ND.

- L. Ron Hubbard's Writers of the Future Contest: quarterly (since 1984). First prize £640 each quarter – plus £2,500 awarded annually for SF, fantasy or horror stories up to 10,000 words. Prizewinners invited to series of writers' workshops.

  Details: Andrea Grant-Webb (Administrator), PO Box 218, East Grinstead, West Sussex, RH19 4GH.

- The Mathew Prichard Award for Short Story Writing: annually. Closing date end-February. First prize £1,200. (Organised by the South and Mid-Wales Association of Writers – SAMWAW – see also page 149.)

  Details: Competition Secretary, The Mathew Prichard Award, 2 Rhododendron Close, Cyncoed, Cardiff CF2 7HS.

- *The New Writer* Prose & Poetry Prizes (see below). Closing date 30th November. Total prize money £2,500. Short stories, serials/novellas, essays, articles and interviews.

  Details: The New Writer, PO Box 60, Cranbrook, Kent TN17 2ZR.

  Website: www.thenewwriter.com

- *Peninsular*, the short story magazine from Cherrybite Publications (see page 114) runs regular open competitions; the top three stories are published in the magazine and the winner is decided by a readers' vote. First prize £200. Details: Cherrybite Publications, Linden Cottage, 45 Burton Road, Little Neston, Cheshire CH64 4AE.

Several other publications – the writing magazines, several of the women's magazines, occasionally some of the newspaper supplements – also run story-writing competitions from time to time. These competitions are announced in the pages of the magazine/paper – details are seldom released in advance.

Several of the small independent press magazines also run short story competitions – often for subscribers only. These magazines come and go: details of their competitions are best found in the market newsletters referred to above.

Poetry competitions

There are many poetry competitions - and the prizes are often excellent. The following list is inevitably incomplete. As with short story competitions, watch the writing magazines – and the market newsletters (see page 157) – for details of forthcoming poetry competitions.

- The Arvon Foundation International Poetry Competition: biennial (since 1980). First prize £5,000.

  Details: The Arvon Foundation, 2nd Floor, 42A Buckingham Palace Road, London SW1W 0RE. Tel: 020 7931 7611. Fax: 020 7963 0961.

  Website: www.arvonfoundation.org

- The Bridport Prize: annually (since 1980). Closing date end-June. First prize £3,000.

  Details - as for short story competition, above.

- Forward Press Top 100 Poets of the Year: annually (since 1998). Closing date end-October. All poems published in the year by the several Forward Press imprints are considered for publication in the Top 100 anthology. First prize £3,000. No entry fees.

  Details: Forward Press Top 100 Information, address on page 2 herein.

- Petra Kenney Poetry Prize: annually (since 1995). Closing date 1 December. First prize £1,000.

  Details: Petra Kenney Poetry Prize, *Writers' Forum*, PO Box 3229, Bournemouth BH1 1ZS.

- Kent & Sussex Poetry Society Open Poetry Competition: annually (since 1985). Closing date end-January. First prize £500.

  Details: Organiser, 13 Ruscombe Close, Southborough, Tunbridge Wells, Kent TN4 0SG.

- The National Poetry Competition: annually. Closing date end-October. First prize £5,000. One of the major open poetry competitions.

  Details: Competition Organiser, The Poetry Society, 22 Betterton Street, London WC2H 9BU.

  Website: www.poetrysoc.com

- *The New Writer* Poetry Competition for single poems (first prize £100) and poetry collections (first prize £300).

  Details as above under Short Story Competitions.

- Peterloo Poets Open Poetry Competition: annually (since 1986). Closing date 1 March. First prize £2,000.

  Details: Peterloo Poets, 2 Kelly Gardens, Calstock, Cornwall PL18 9SA.

- Ver Poets Open Competition: annually. Closing date end-April. Total prizes about £1,000.

  Details: Organiser, 61-63 Chiswell Green Lane, St Albans, Herts AL2 3AL.

✓

10-Point Checklist ... on Competitions

✓ Write what is asked for. For example, it's no good sending an article, an essay, a personal experience or a narrative poem to a short story competition. A short story is a piece of prose fiction. Anything else will be disqualified. If the short story competition calls for a ghost story, write a ghost story. Don't send in that sci-fi tale or that romantic fable you've just finished – if it isn't a ghost story it will be thrown out.

✓ If the winning entry is to be published in a magazine, read several issues of the relevant publication. Make sure your entry is suitable. Don't ruin your chances by using inappropriate language or subject matter.

✓ Respect the stipulated length limits absolutely. Make sure your entry observes any minimum and/or maximum wordage limits stated in the rules. An experienced judge will spot lengths under or over those required, and will check the count. Count the words. Don't rely on computer word counts.

✓ Use standard manuscript layout. For prose: double line spacing, good margins all round, plain roman type on white A4 paper. Keep paragraph indents consistent. For poetry: single line spacing in stanzas, double line space between stanzas. Don't use italic or condensed types or a small point size; judges loathe these eye-strainers. Make sure your ribbon or printer produces clear black easy-to-read type. (NB: 'double spacing' means one full line of white space between lines of type, not half a line of space. It doesn't mean two spaces between words, either.)

✔ Present a clean, clear, crisp typescript. Don't send a script that has handwritten inserts or corrections, blobs of correction fluid or overtyped words. Retype the whole thing rather than send in a heavily corrected script. First impressions count.

✔ Don't use fancy folders, bindings or decorated title pages. These are an unnecessary nuisance and a distraction. (And, by some strange law of probability, judges find that the most elaborate presentation always seems to contain the poorest writing.)

✔ If the competition rules require you to write under a pseudonym, observe the instructions. If you ignore such regulations and give yourself a byline, your entry will be disqualified. (And make sure that **only** your pseudonym appears anywhere on the submitted entry.)

✔ Be sure to allow yourself enough time to re-read your entry for typos, spelling mistakes and incorrect syntax. Don't ruin your chances through carelessness.

✔ If the rules require you to state a target market for your entry – for example, the competition is for an article and you are asked to state the magazine for which it is written – be sure to do this. You might consider your entry to be suitable for any magazine, but you must still comply with the rules. And don't forget to check that the publication you name is one that accepts contributions.

✔ Get your entry in on time. If you miss the closing date, your entry will be disqualified and you'll have done all that work for nothing. Don't leave it till the last minute.

To summarise - comply with competition rules, or don't enter.

12

UPDATING MARKET INFORMATION

No other book offers the same depth of detailed information about potential markets for 'ordinary' freelance writers as does this Handbook, especially now we can keep you up to date on the information featured in this edition through our new e-mail update service (see below). But inevitably, even this book gradually becomes out-of-date with the passage of time. You need to be business-like in working at keeping it up-dated from other sources as well.

There has recently been a significant reduction in the number of writing magazines published in Britain. Details of the remaining writing magazines that pay for contributions are included in Chapter 1; they offer quite a lot of market information in various forms.

There are also two publications that specialise in offering up-to-date information on magazine markets. Because they themselves are not really in the market for freelance contributions, they are not listed in Chapter 1. They are:

- *Freelance Market News*: £2.64 per issue. (Notional price.) Available on subscription only, 11 issues per year (not July) for £29 (or £17 for 6 issues), from: Writers' Bureau, Sevendale House, 7 Dale Street, Manchester M1 1JB. Tel: 0161 228 2362, extension 210. E-mail: fmn@writersbureau.com

Write, phone or e-mail for a free sample copy.

Each issue has 16 A4 pages listing mainly magazine (but some book publishers, too) markets both in the UK and overseas, giving details of their requirements, editorial staff and address changes, also specific details of (paid) letter and other 'filler' opportunities. News of open competitions – and also of their own monthly competition details and results. (They publish their competition winners – short stories, articles, poetry – in the magazine too.) They also frequently include an in-depth study of one magazine's requirements and sometimes an article about opportunities in a specific writing market area, bought-in and paid for, at 'rate A'.

Freelance Market News has been around in various guises since 1968; it always used to be THE market newsletter – but now it has competition.

- *Writers' Bulletin*: £2.00 per issue. Available by post only, 4 issues per year – subscribe for as many issues as you wish, from Cherrybite Publications, Linden Cottage. 45 Burton Road, Little Neston, Cheshire CH64 4AE. (Cheques payable to Cherrybite Publications.)

Founded by Chriss McCallum, *Writers' Bulletin* is now compiled, edited, produced and published by Shelagh Nugent. The magazine proudly boasts that every item in it is verified at source before publication.

Each issue has 32 A5 pages listing details of new and changing 'mainstream' magazines and their editorial staff and requirements, similar details of new (usually small) publishers, similar details of some of the larger small (independent) press magazines, forthcoming courses and writers' conferences, imminent closing dates for open competitions, and relevant (usually how-to) book reviews. There is usually an in-depth review of the requirements of at least one magazine or publisher. Unlike *Freelance Market News*, *Writers' Bulletin* excludes almost everything other than market and competition information, and an occasional article (always commissioned) on some aspect of writing; there are no own competitions, no judges' commentaries, no winning poems or stories.

Take your choice – both are good. And, for up-to-date, down to earth and ruthlessly honest reviews and information about Small Press magazines, try *Dragon's Breath*, a monthly print newsletter at an amazingly good price: £2.50 for 12 issues in the UK (£4.50 Europe, £7.80 RoW), cheques payable to Tony Lee. *Dragon's Breath* is published by Pigasus Press, 13 Hazely Coombe, Arreton, Isle of Wight PO30 3AJ. You can read current and back issues of *Dragon's Breath* online at http:freespace.virgin.net/pigasus.press/dragonsbreath.html

You can choose from hundreds of Small Press magazines in the annual *Small Press Guide*, published by Writers' Bookshop, the publishers of this Handbook. Their address is on page 2.

And don't forget *The Fix* (see page 112) for reviews of independent magazines, and the invaluable *Light's List* (see page 107).

The Magazine Writer's Handbook e-mail update service

The wonderful technology of e-mail allows us to offer, for the first time, a FREE update service on the information included in this 9th edition of the Handbook. All you have to do is send your name and your e-mail address to Chriss McCallum at **Magwriter9@aol.com** typing 'Ninth edition updates' in the subject line.

Our promise: We will keep any information you give us about yourself, including your e-mail address, absolutely confidential. **Nothing will be passed on to anyone else** at any time for any purpose whatsoever.

13

ADDRESSES USEFUL TO THE FREELANCE WRITER

Freelance non-fiction writers depend on information (and personal experience) to keep them writing. And, as mentioned in Chapter 10, they can benefit from associating with other writers.

This chapter lists some useful but less than widely known research sources/addresses for acquiring information.

Remaindered ('bargain') books

Every serious freelance writer of non-fiction builds up a personal reference library. Inevitably, your 'library' will contain many specialist books relevant to your particular area of interest. Don't forget the various shops selling *remaindered* books, like 'The Works' and similar publishers' outlets, when you're searching for such books. A book of narrow interest may not sell well, and may therefore quickly be remaindered; but these are often the books of most value to the freelance writer who specialises in the particular subject.

There are two major mail-order retail sellers of remaindered books; both will, on request, add your name to their mailing list. I have dealt with both and had excellent service. They are:

- **Bibliophile Books**, 5 Thomas Road, London E14 7BN. For queries or credit card orders, tel: 020 7515 9222; fax: 020 7538 4115; or, 24-hour answer-phone for credit card orders, 020 7515 9555.

  Bibliophile charge a flat fee of £3.00 per UK order (any number of books) for postage and packing – but for surface mail despatch of overseas orders, add postage at £1.50 (Europe), £2.00 (North America), £2.50 (Middle East) or £3.00 (Rest of the World) per book. (Check with them for overseas air mail postage.)

- **Postscript**, 24 Langroyd Road, London SW17 7PL. For queries or credit card orders, tel: 020-8767 7421 during office hours; outside office hours, answer-phone on 020-8682 0280; fax at any time on 020-8682 0280.

  Postscript charge a flat fee per order for postage and packing for any number of books despatched to anywhere in UK/Eire; and they offer 'economy' overseas despatch rates. Contact them for current rates and overseas air mail postage costs.

Press cuttings

The serious non-fiction writer collects other people's articles and news cuttings relevant to his or her specialist interests. A browse through your collection of cuttings can often spark off an idea for a fresh general-interest article. And you can never get enough cuttings.

There are press cutting agencies which, for a fee, will provide you with newspaper clippings of all the reviews of your latest book. These agencies are of interest but little use to the magazine writer.

Other than for purposes of amassing a personal collection, however, the acquisition of print cuttings has been made unnecessary by the Internet. With a few clicks of the mouse, you can find more information than you could cope with in a lifetime. Free access is available to reliable sources like the British Library and the *CIA World Factbook*. (See Chapter 15 on The Internet for some of the best websites for writers.)

Associations

- **Arts Council of England**, 14 Great Peter Street, London SW1P 3NQ. General tel: 020 7973 6517. E-mail: enquiries@artscouncil.org.uk

  The national policy body of the arts in England. Incorporates the English regional arts boards. **Live Literature** contact: Hilary Davidson, tel: 020 7973 6442.

  Live Literature website: www.liveliterature.net

- **Association of Christian Writers**: contact the Administrator, Mrs. Jenny Kyriacou, All Saints Vicarage, 43 All Saints Close, Edmonton, London N9 9AT. Tel/fax: 020 8884 4348. E-mail: admin@christianwriters.org.uk

  Website: www.aswin.uklinux.net/ACW

  Offers many benefits for Christian writers. Membership includes a resource pack, a quarterly magazine, *Candle & Keyboard*, access to manuscript criticism, area group meetings and postal workshops, Writers' Days, and a biennial conference.

- **Bureau of Freelance Photographers**, Focus House, 497 Green Lanes, London N13 4BP. Tel: 020 8882 3315. E-mail: info@thebfp.com

  A commercial organisation principally for photographers and photo-journalists wishing to improve their craft and market their work. Has many benefits of use to the freelance writer. Membership (currently £45.00 per year UK, £60.00 RoW – reduced rates for 3-year and 5-year subscriptions) includes the annual *Freelance Photographer's Market Handbook* (see page 168), a monthly full-colour *Market Newsletter* giving regular updates on all the *Handbook* entries, and access to a highly efficient free advisory service.

- **National Association of Writers' Groups (NAWG)**. Headquarters: The Arts Centre, Biddick Lane, Washington, Tyne & Wear NE38 2AB. All correspondence should be addressed to Diane Wilson, Secretary NAWG, Suite Two, 23 Cambridge Street, Bridlington, East Yorkshire YO16 4JY. Tel/fax: 01262 609228. E-mail: mikediane@tesco.net

  Website: www.nawg.co.uk

  A UK-wide association of writers' groups. At the time of writing, membership stands at 140 groups and 80 associate (individual) members – and growing. Provides an information service on where to find a writers' group and how to set one up from scratch. Runs free entry competitions for members, and an annual 3-day Open Festival of Writing (alternating August/September), open to both members and non-members, at St Aidan's College, Durham University.

Publishes a bi-monthly 28-page newsletter, *Link*, edited by Mike Wilson; *Link* is available on subscription to individuals, whether members of a writers' group or not (groups have special terms). Individual subscriptions cost £7.00 a year. The newsletter has news of member groups, with a focus on a particular group in each issue, articles on various aspects of writing and getting published, information about writing competitions run by member groups, and a lively exchange of views in its letters page.

- **National Union of Journalists**, Headland House, 308-312 Gray's Inn Road, London WC1X 8DP. Tel: 020 7278 7916. Fax: 020 7837 8143. E-mail: info@huj.org.uk

  Website: www.nuj.org.uk

  The journalists' trade union. Membership includes the union's magazine *The Journalist*, which is available to non-members for a subscription of £20.00 a year (10 issues).

- **Society of Authors**. Contact: Membership Secretary, 84 Drayton Gardens, London SW10 9SB. Tel: 020-7373 6642.

  Join as soon as a publisher accepts your book, but before you sign the contract.

- **Society of Civil and Public Service Writers**. Contact: Mrs J. M. Hykin, 17 The Green, Corby Glen, Grantham, Lincs NG33 4NP.

  Open to past and present members of the Civil Service and some other public bodies and aims to encourage all forms of writing.)

- **Society of Women Writers and Journalists**. Contact: Jean Hawkes, 110 Whitehall Road, London E4 6DW. Tel: 020-8529 0886.

  Founded in 1894, the SWWJ – as it is known to all – holds monthly lunch-time meetings/lectures in London, and has several active regional sections.

And an agency for short stories

Midland Exposure, 4 Victoria Court, Oadby, Leicester LE2 4AF. Tel: 0116 271 8332; fax: 0116 281 2188. E-mail: partners@midlandexposure.co.uk Website: www.midlandexposure.co.uk

Midland Exposure is an agency specialising in short fiction for women's magazines. Run by Cari Crook and Lesley Gleeson, two well-published writers who know their market well, Midland Exposure is an established agency which is held in high regard by editors of women's magazines throughout the UK.

Cari and Lesley write: 'We are an agency selling short fiction to all the weekly women's magazines, including those not taking unsolicited fiction.

'We charge a reading fee for each script submitted, up to 2,500 words. Please contact us for our current rates. If a story is accepted into the agency, its reading fee is refunded. Once you have a story accepted, reading fees are no longer charged.

'Our commission charges are: 25% on first five sales, 20% on next five, and 15% thereafter.

'For further details and a comprehensive set of guidelines, send an s.a.e. to the address above, e-mail us, or browse our website.'

14
THE MAGAZINE WRITER'S BOOKSHELF

It is always difficult to recommend books for others, whose needs and tastes are never the same as one's own. Nevertheless, there are some books associated with or about writing for magazines that are fairly standard in their acceptance; and there are others we believe are worth looking at. Listed below are those we think are the best (including, of course, some of our own). There are others that might suit you better, but at least have a look at these.

Standard reference books

Every writer needs a good dictionary. We recommend either:

The Chambers Dictionary (Chambers). Comprehensive and user-friendly (Chriss's favourite); or **The Concise Oxford Dictionary** (OUP). Some consider it too academic but when you get to know it it's easy to work with. (Gordon prefers this one.)

The Oxford Dictionary for Writers & Editors (OUP, newest edition, 2000). Unbeatable for sorting out the preferred choice from alternative spellings and when to use capital letters, hyphens, etc. It is also excellent on punctuation and on printing terms, and on unusual names of people and places.

Roget's Thesaurus (Penguin). Good to refer to, but avoid over-use.

Collins Gem Thesaurus (Collins). Pocket-sized, quicker to use than Roget's (but, of course, less comprehensive); particularly useful too for its foreign phrases, and its list of Christian names.

Pears Cyclopedia (Penguin). Updated annually.

The Penguin Encyclopedia (Penguin). An ideal one-volume 'first source'.

Everyman's Encyclopaedia (J. M. Dent). Marvellous: try second-hand shops.

The Wordsworth Encyclopedia (Wordsworth). Ideal, and the best value of all – five paperback volumes for a tenner.

The Cambridge Biographical Encyclopedia (Cambridge UP). International and up-to-date – and covers both the dead and the living.

Ann Hoffmann: **Research for Writers** (A. & C. Black). The 'standard'. Ideal for authors of biographical and historical books; useful to all non-fiction writers; more than most fiction writers will need.

The Writers' & Artists' Yearbook (A. & C. Black, annually).

The Writer's Handbook (Macmillan/PEN, annually).

These two annual reference works cover an immense range of publications and publishers: they can, therefore, include only limited information about each. One or the other is essential for every freelance writer: but both need to be supplemented by this more detailed Handbook.

Writing for magazines

Donna Baker: **How to Write Stories for Magazines** (Allison & Busby). Helpful, clear, easy to read. Ideal for short story beginners.

Alison Chisholm: **How to Write Five-Minute Features** (Allison & Busby). Detailed advice by an expert money-making letter- and filler-writer.

Alison Chisholm and Brenda Courtie: **How to Write about Yourself** (Allison & Busby). How to draw on your personal experience for articles and short stories.

Joan Clayton: **Journalism for Beginners** and **Interviewing for Journalists** (both Piatkus). Comprehensive introduction to the essential skills.

Jill Dick: **Writing for Magazines** and **Freelance Writing for Newspapers** (A & C Black 'Writing' series). Excellent handbooks by a highly experienced journalist.

Greg Daugherty: **You Can Write for Magazines** (Writers' Digest Books, USA). Enthusiastic, encouraging, American – one of the many excellent books for writers from this US publisher – available from larger bookshops or from Amazon.co.uk online.

Jane Dorner: **The Internet: A Writer's Guide** (A & C Black). Comprehensive guide by a well qualified writer, looking at the Internet from the writer's point of view.

Peter Finch: **How to Publish Your Poetry** (Allison & Busby). Absolutely the best on its subject; covers publishing poetry in magazines, books, pamphlets and on the internet.

John Hines: **The Way to Write Magazine Articles** (Elm Tree Books). Practical advice on article-writing: a different approach from Gordon's (see below).

Chriss McCallum: **Getting Published** (How To Books). A concise introduction to the art of getting into print, based on Chriss's 40-plus years in the publishing business, both in-house and freelance.

Chriss McCallum: **Writing for Publication** (How To Books). One of the very best 'across the board' books for beginning writers; down-to-earth and practical. Now in its fourth, successful edition.

John Morrison: **Freelancing for Magazines** (BFP Books, London). A comprehensive guide for writers and photographers, packed with practical advice. Published by the Bureau of Freelance Photographers – see page 162.

Hank Nuwer: **How to Write Like an Expert About Anything** (Writer's Digest Books). Practical advice on giving your writing the ring of authority, whatever your topic.

Iain Pattison: **Cracking The Short Story Market** (Writers' Bureau). Simply excellent – should become a standard. A really good read, too.

Adèle Ramet: **Writing Short Stories & Articles** (How To Books). Useful guidance for both newcomers and established writers.

Jean Saunders: **Writing Step by Step** (Allison & Busby). Good general advice on all aspects of writing from a prolific and very successful writer of romantic novels and short stories. Best on fiction.

Dave Taylor: **A Guide to Comicscripting** (Robert Hale). The only book on the market about writing picture-script – and excellent too. It's all in pictures.

John Tracy & Stewart Gibson (Eds): **The Freelance Photographer's Market Handbook** (BFP Books, London). Annual markets handbook published by the Bureau of Freelance Photographers (see page 162). How and where to sell photographs and articles. Includes trade and industry magazines not covered in the other main directories.

Gordon Wells: **The Craft of Writing Articles** (Allison & Busby). A step-by-step beginners' guide to writing saleable magazine articles. The best: and now in its second edition.

Gordon Wells: **Writing: The Hobby that Pays** (EPB Publishers, Singapore). We think this is THE best general book for beginners. It is based on Gordon's 40-plus years of writing and selling. (Available direct from him at 43 Broomfield Road, Henfield, West Sussex BN5 9UD. £8.50 post free.)

Stella Whitelaw: **How to Write Short-short Stories** (Allison & Busby). More and more magazines are asking for one-page stories. These *short-shorts* require a different technique to conventional short stories. Stella tells all.

Sally-Jayne Wright: **How to Write and Sell Interviews** (Allison & Busby). Excellent step-by-step, practical advice on one of the most important techniques for non-fiction research and writing.

Writing style

William Strunk Jr & E B White, **The Elements of Style** (Longman): To settle all those doubts about grammar and syntax.

Keith Waterhouse: **Waterhouse on Newspaper Style** (Viking hb, Penguin pb). Probably the best book of all time on good writing style for newspapers - and equally relevant to writing for popular magazines. A good read too. Get it, even if it takes your last penny.

15

THE INTERNET FOR WRITERS

There's a revolution going on in the world of writing. It's called the Internet, and you have much to gain from the changes it's bringing. Welcome it, embrace it, and use it – wisely.

Above all, don't be afraid of it. It can look big and scary from the outside, but it's pretty user-friendly, and once you get into it you'll wonder how you ever managed without it.

The Internet is **not** a universal replacement for the writing life we're all familiar with. We still need, and will continue to need for the foreseeable future, the phone, the fax, the post, the library, the bookshop, the writers' associations, the personal contacts ...

The Internet is a marvellous resource and a wonderfully useful tool, but it isn't a magic wand – it's still a tool, to be used by you, the individual writer, in ways best suited to your particular needs.

So What is the Internet?

Put simply, the Internet is a worldwide network of interlinked computers which can communicate with each other to share information. Think of a super-sophisticated telephone system that's able to store *and* transmit not only speech but also text, pictures, sound and video. With a home computer and a modem, you can tap into this vast system and use it both to communicate with others and to access information sources *anywhere in the world*. The Internet recognises no borders, no boundaries.

(A modem is a connecting device – many computers have one built in, some require a small piece of external equipment.)

You can get on to the Internet through many public libraries and 'cybercafés', but this can be frustrating if you need frequent access or want to read or send e-mail at times when these places are closed. Ideally, you should have your own computer and modem.

Access to the Internet is usually made through an Internet Service Provider (ISP) – there are dozens to choose from. Some offer free access, but if you're a complete novice these can cost you dearly because of high charges for any help you might need (some help-lines charge as much as £1 per minute). There are ISPs who, in return for a monthly fee, offer free or very cheap help facilities, both online and by telephone; one of these would probably be a wiser choice if you're a beginner. There are many magazines on general sale which give information on ISPs, with regular updates on services and charges. You could save yourself a lot of headaches – and money – by reading some of these before you sign up.

For general information about the Internet and how to get connected and find your way around, I recommend *The Rough Guide to the Internet* by Angus Kennedy (Rough Guides – make sure you read the latest edition). There are several books about the Internet written specifically for writers. One of the best is *The Internet: A Writer's Guide* by Jane Dorner (A & C Black). But hands-on experience is the best way to learn. You'll soon find plenty of links to writing sites – there are more than you could ever hope to look at.

The two functions of the Internet which are of particular interest to writers are the World Wide Web and e-mail.

The World Wide Web

The World Wide Web (abbreviation www) holds to the principle of universal readership: all information published on the Internet must be accessible by anyone from anywhere. Once you've grasped that concept, you'll soon feel completely at ease reading, say, this morning's online edition of *The San Francisco Chronicle* then flicking, a click on an on-screen button, to London's *Evening Standard* or Paris's *Le Monde*.

The World Wide Web is a collection of websites: a website is a collection of linked pages under a single domain name known as a URL (Unique Reference Locator). URL addresses begin with the protocol http:// usually followed by www then the specific domain address. This sounds complicated but you'll soon get used to the long strings of letters that make up web addresses. More and more, the http:// prefix is becoming a 'given' and is being omitted from printed addresses. Web addresses *must* be keyed in accurately; an approximation won't do – even a single wrong character will result in your request not being recognised.

To access Web pages, you sign on to your ISP, then locate your required URL via a search engine like, for example, Yahoo or Webcrawler. My own favourite is Google; it's fast, efficient and easy to follow.

To make life easier, most search engines also respond to 'normal' language – try keying, for example, 'Romance magazines USA' into your search engine's address line, click the 'Search' or 'Find' button and marvel at the lists of links to American magazine websites that will appear on your screen.

For the magazine writer, then, there's a rich seam of information and resources to be mined on the Web, as well as opportunities to promote yourself and your work:

- Research: you can gather information on your subject from websites around the world. Remember, though, that the Internet is unregulated and anyone, individuals or companies, can publish anything they like on the Web, so be wary of self-styled experts. Double-check information you get from any source you suspect might be less than impeccable.

- Markets: you can find markets for your writing all over the English-speaking world. Thousands of magazines now publish online editions, and many magazine websites also include guidelines for writing for their print editions.

- Links: once you've found your way on to the 'writers' net' you can get involved, if you wish, with the worldwide writers' community; you can contact people with the same interests as yourself, discuss problems, exchange information, curse editors … it's up to you how far you want to take the contacts you make.

- E-zines (often called webzines): these are small-press-type magazines which might be produced solely online or with a corresponding print version. Some are freely accessible, others require a subscription. Some you can read on-screen, others come to you via e-mail and can be saved to a file in your word-processing program so you can read them offline at your leisure. There are e-zines about every imaginable subject, some so specialised they would have little chance of appearing in general magazines, and there are many e-zines about writing and the writing life. You'll find them easily by following links given in the 'writing' websites. To read some e-zines, you might need to download Adobe Acrobat Reader, which is easily available, free, from the Adobe website (see below).

- Your own website: most ISPs offer space for you to set up your own website, to promote yourself and your work in any way you wish. For example, you could display samples of your published work (provided you've kept the copyright) and offer your services as a freelance writer in your particular field.

- Other people's websites: many websites offer the opportunity for writers to promote themselves, usually in return for a fee or for a service you can provide in exchange.

E-mail

This is one of the greatest boons the electronic age has brought for the writer. It's fast and it's cheap and, unlike phones and faxes, it doesn't interrupt you in the middle of something crucial. Most ISPs allow you to have anything from one to seven password-protected e-mail addresses where you can send and receive electronic messages – particularly useful if you write under one or more pen-names.

You can write your e-mail messages offline, i.e. before you connect to your ISP, and send them anywhere in the world when you're ready, for the cost of a local phone call. You can even send the same message to any number of people at the same time for no extra cost. You can also instruct your server to send your e-mails out during off-peak rates.

With e-mail, you enjoy the speed of the telephone while retaining a copy of your message and a record of when you sent it. Since many editors are now happy to look at ideas submitted by e-mail, and will often reply a lot quicker than they do with 'snail-mail', you can save a lot of 'waiting-for-the-post' time. E-mail is also invaluable for sorting out those close-to-deadline queries on accepted work.

Another bonus of e-mail is that you can sign up to receive newsletters from organisations in your field of interest, delivered regularly to your electronic mailbox and very often totally free of charge to you, the costs of setting up and maintaining these services being met by advertising.

Useful websites

Here are just a few useful websites operating at the time of writing (Web addresses ending in .com are usually US-based. British sites usually end in '.co.uk' or, for some charitable organisations, '.org.uk'):

Adobe Acrobat Reader - Free to download facility enabling web documents to be read on-screen: http://www.adobe.com/products/acrobat/readstep.html

American news-stand magazines listings: http://www.enews.com

Audit Bureau of Circulation (ABC) – information and circulation figures about major UK magazines: www.abc.org.uk

The BBC (access to all departments): http://www.bbc.co.uk

Biography.com - all the latest news on the rich and famous: www.biography.com

The British Library (access to all departments and research facilities): http://www.bl.uk

BT Directory Enquiries – free access to all BT directories online: www.bt.com/directory-enquiries/dq_home.jsp

Children's Writing Resource Centre (US): http://www.write4kids.com

CIA World Factbook – Country by country information on just about everything you need to know, with illustrative graphs and maps; includes Geography, People, Government, Economy, Communications, Transportation, Military etc.: www.cia.gov/cia/publications/factbook

Crime Writers' Association: http://www.twbooks.co.uk/cwa/cwa.html

International Journalists' Network: http://www.ijnet.org

Journalism UK – valuable research site for article writers: www.journalismuk.co.uk

The National Union of Journalists: http://www.gn.apc.org/media/nuj.html

The Poetry Business – Organisation publishing a literary magazine, running an annual Book and Pamphlet competition, plus writing days: www.poetrybusiness.co.uk

The Poetry Kit – Lists poetry competitions, events, interviews, magazines, courses, workshops, publishers etc. worldwide: www.poetrykit.org

The Poetry Society: www.poetrysociety.org

The *Press Gazette* – The weekly publication covering newspaper and magazine news from the UK and around the world: http://www.pressgazette.co.uk

The Society of Authors: http://www.writers.org.uk/society

WriteLink – Site with links to paying markets, competitions, reference sites etc.: www.writelink.dabsol.co.uk

Writer's Digest (US magazine) – Brilliant source of advice, articles on writing, and writers' guidelines for a multitude of publications: http://www.writersdigest.com

The Writers' Guild of Great Britain: http://www.writers.org.uk/guild

The Writer's Internet Resource Guide: http://novalearn.com/wirg/

Writers Write (large online resource): http://www.writerswrite.com

Writing-World – Large resource site with many links, also offering a free regular newsletter; well worth a look: www.writing-world.com

And, as a taster, a trio of interesting, attractively set-up and easy to navigate e-zines:

LITERARY POTPOURRI

Editor-in Chief: Beverly Jackson

E-mail: jacksonwrites@cox.net

Website: www.literarypotpourri.com

Postal address: PO Box 1034, Blue Lake, CA 95525, USA.

Literary Potpourri publishes a wide mix of material, which must be original and unpublished:

- Short stories – 6,000 words maximum, prefers 1,000 to 3,500 words
- Flash fiction – 1,000 words maximum
- Poetry – Preferably under 100 lines
- Essays/memoirs – on any subject, but must be well written and carry a fresh point of view
- Book reviews – see website for details.

From June 2002, *Literary Potpourri* is able to pay its contributors, thanks to sales of its print anthologies and to the generosity of its corporate sponsor Levenger.

They ask for First North American Serial Rights and First Electronic Rights, plus certain other rights – see website for details.

You can submit material either by e-mail or by post (in which case you need to enclose the Writer's Form included on the Online Submissions page.

Literary Potpourri does **not** want mainstream Christian, Women's Fiction, Romance or Science Fiction genres.

Spend some time at the website before you offer any material, to see the quality of the work accepted by *Literary Potpourri*. The standard is high.

PATCHWORD – The Online Writers' Resource

Editor: Gwyneth Box

E-mail: editor@patchword.com

Website: www.patchword.com

Postal Address: Calle Carlos Arniches, 7 – 2D, Madrid 28005, Spain.

Patchword includes

- A poetry anthology – includes classical and contemporary poems, and poetry in translation

- Articles about all aspects of writing

- Book Reviews (all genres)

- Non-fiction and writing for children

- Fiction – short or excerpts – occasionally included as Editor's Choice

- Small ads and competitions listing

- A time-out section with quizzes, games, trivia, quotes etc.

Since there is currently no payment for contributions, *Patchword* is happy to accept reprints. Submissions are welcome from published and non-published writers anywhere in the world. Full guidelines are available on the website.

E-mail submissions are greatly preferred – please include text in the body of the e-mail unless previous arrangements have been made to send attached files.

STRIDE MAGAZINE

Editor: Rupert Loydell

E-mail: editor@stridemagazine.co.uk (for queries) or submissions@stridemagazine.co.uk (for submissions)

Website: www.stridemagazine.co.uk

Postal address: Stride Magazine, 11 Sylvan Road, Exeter, Devon EX4 6EW.

After 33 years as a poetry magazine, four issues as an 'occasional arts journal', and a few years gap, *Stride* is now reincarnated as a webzine.

Stride publishes:

- New poetry
- Short prose
- Articles
- News
- Reviews – 'and whatever takes our fancy'.

The Editor welcomes submissions of 4 or 5 poems, short prose, reviews or articles. Please submit in the body of e-mails (**not** attachments) to submissions@stridemagazine.co.uk. Or you can send submissions by snail-mail (with s.a.e. for reply) to the address above.

Copyright of everything submitted remains with the author. *Stride* does not pay for material, but promises your work will be seen by thousands of readers!

BASIC GLOSSARY
of Terms Commonly Used in Magazine Publishing

Acceptance: An offer from an editor to publish submitted work.

Advertorial: A 'feature' focusing on a company or product; the words 'advertising feature' or 'advertisement feature' usually appear at the top of the page.

Article: A (usually short) piece of journalistic writing.

Artwork: Illustrations, photographs, ornamental lettering, fancy headings – pretty much anything that isn't part of the text.

Assignment: A request to a freelance from an editor to produce material on a specific subject; wordage, angle, fee, and possibly a kill fee are usually agreed in advance.

Boxed item: Factual information (contact addresses, phone numbers etc.) supporting a feature and often printed in a frame. Sometimes called a sidebar or text box.

Bullets: Large dots preceding and adding emphasis to lines or paragraphs, often used to distinguish lists of points in a feature. Indicated with asterisks in mss.

Byline: A line under the title or at the end of a piece, identifying the writer, eg 'by William Shakespeare'.

©: A symbol signifying that a work is protected by copyright.

Caption: The text identifying or explaining a picture.

Circulation: Total number of copies distributed.

Commissioned article: An article written to the order of an editor who promises to buy the finished piece at an agreed price.

Consumer magazine: A magazine covering general affairs, sports, hobbies etc. rather than business, trade and professional matters.

The Magazine Writer's Handbook

Copy: Term used throughout publishing for matter which is to be typeset.

Contributor's copy: A copy of the magazine issue in which the writer's work appears. Often the only 'payment' offered by 'small presses'.

Copyright: The exclusive right in his or her own work of a writer or other designated party, as defined in law.

Copywriting: Writing material for use in advertisements, publicity material and suchlike.

Cover mount: Free gift attached to a magazine cover.

Deadline: Date (and possibly time) by which a finished piece must be submitted.

Defamation: Damage to someone's name or reputation. See also 'Libel'.

Draft: A preliminary version.

DTP = desktop publishing: Computer programs used to design pages (text and pictures) on screen instead of pasting up on paper. QuarkXpress and PageMaker are used by many publishers.

Editorial: 1. Introductory column, usually written by the editor. 2. Text other than advertising copy.

Expenses: The money it costs you to research and write your article or feature. Some editors (but by no means all) pay expenses on top of the agreed rate for the work.

Fact: A reality as distinct from an idea or belief.

Faction: Writing which blurs the distinction between fact and fiction.

FBSR = First British Serial Rights: The right to publish a piece for the first time and once only in the UK.

Feature: A piece of journalism that deals with a topic in depth but is not one of a series.

Format: Size, shape and general layout.

Freebie: Anything given free, often samples given in the hope of favourable publicity.

Guidelines/Writers' Guidelines: Detailed specification of editorial requirements.

Hard copy: Copy printed out on paper.

Hook: A strong beginning to grab and hold the reader's attention.

House style: The agreed and/or evolved style in which a publication is produced, eg '-ise' or '-ize' endings, italics or roman type for book and film titles, single or double quotation marks; the details that keep a publication's overall style consistent and recognisable. Usually set out in a style book or sheet.

Human interest: Material about people, their achievements, problems, ambitions, social and economic circumstances etc.

In-house Work done or ideas generated by the publication's own staff.

Intro (abbreviation of 'Introduction'): The opening paragraph of a feature or article, possibly printed in a bigger or bolder type than the body of the text. Designed to capture the reader.

IRC = International Reply Coupon: A voucher sold at post offices worldwide, equivalent to the value of the minimum postal rate for a letter from the country from which the reply is to be sent.

Justified setting/justification: The spacing out of words so that each line of text is the same length, flush left and right.

Kill fee: Fee paid to a writer when a commissioned piece is not used.

Layout: The overall appearance of the pages of a publication.

Lead: Journalistic term referring to the opening of a news story or magazine article.

Lead time: The time between the copy date and the date of publication.

Leader: A principal piece in a newspaper or magazine, a main story or article.

Libel: A statement, written, printed or broadcast in any medium, which defames an identifiable living person by holding them up to hatred, ridicule or contempt.

Line art: Artwork entirely in black on white with no varied tones.

Market study: Analytical study of possible points of sale.

Media: Sources of information (newspapers, magazines, TV etc.). Plural of 'medium of communication'.

Ms/manuscript: The typewritten or word-processed text you send to the editor.

Moral right: Introduced in the Copyright, Designs and Patents Act of 1988, Moral Right complements but does not supersede copyright. It gives the writer the right to be identified as the author of his or her own work and prevents anyone else from distorting or mutilating that work. However, unlike the rest of Europe, where Moral Right is undisputed and automatic, in the UK it must be asserted in writing, otherwise it is deemed not to exist.

On spec/on speculation: A piece of work sent to an editor unsolicited or without a promise that it will be bought is described as being sent 'on spec'.

Outline: A sketched-out structure of a piece, showing what it will contain and in what order, but with little or no detail.

PA: Personal Assistant.

Perfect bound: having a spine to which the pages are glued.

Piece: Jargon for any piece of written journalistic work, whether article or feature.

Photo-journalism: Journalism in which the text is of secondary importance to the photographs.

Pic/pix: Jargon for 'picture/pictures'.

Plagiarism: The use without permission, whether deliberate or accidental, of work in which the copyright is held by someone else.

Professional journal: A publication produced specifically for circulation in a particular profession.

Proof: A print-out of the typeset work. Usually (but not always) checked by sub-editors or proofreaders.

Readership: A collective term applied to the people who habitually read a particular publication.

RoW = Rest of the world: Anywhere outside the UK.

Saddle-stitched: Stapled through the back-centre fold.

S.a.e./stamped self-addressed envelope: Customarily enclosed with every submission except commissioned or requested work. Must be large enough and bear sufficient postage for the return of the work. If you omit the s.a.e. you might never see your ms again.

Shout line: A prominent line of text on a magazine cover drawing attention to an important piece inside.

Sidebar: Short feature accompanying a news story or article, enlarging on some aspect of the piece. Usually boxed or set in a different typeface or otherwise distinguished from the main text.

Simultaneous submissions: The same material sent to more than one magazine at a time.

'Snail mail': Normal postal services as distinct from electronic mail.

Stable: A group of writers whose work is regularly commissioned and published by a magazine.

Standfirst: An introductory paragraph in bigger and/or bolder type summarising the content of an article.

Story: Jargon for a feature or an article. Not to be confused with fiction stories.

Submission: Material sent to an editor with a view to publication.

Syndication: Selling the same piece several times over to non-competing publications, possibly in different countries.

Trade journal: A publication produced for circulation among practitioners and companies in a particular trade or industry.

Unsolicited submission: Work sent to an editor without invitation.

Voucher copy: A copy of a single issue of a publication sent free to a writer whose work appears in that issue, as a courtesy and as evidence (to vouch) that the work has in fact been published.

INDEX

Magazines featured in this edition of the *Handbook* as markets are set in bold